Cuisinart Bread Machine Cookbook

Easy and Flavorful Bread Recipes for Beginners, Including Gluten-Free Options, for Family Baking Bliss – 1800 Days of Pure Joy!

Wepold Gightshy

Table of Contents

INTRODUCTION

Things You Need to Know About Your Cuisinart Bread Machine

Your Cuisinart compact automatic bread maker is a versatile kitchen appliance designed to simplify the bread-making process and expand your culinary horizons. Here's everything you need to know about your Cuisinart bread machine:

Ease of Use: The Cuisinart bread maker is designed to be user-friendly, with 12 preprogrammed menu options that cover a wide range of bread types and baking preferences. Whether you're a novice baker or a seasoned pro, you'll find the interface intuitive and easy to navigate.

Customization Options: One of the standout features of the Cuisinart bread maker is its customization options. You can choose from three crust shades—light, medium, or dark—allowing you to tailor each loaf to your desired level of crispiness. Additionally, the machine can bake up to a 2-pound loaf, giving you flexibility in portion size.

Compact Design: The vertical baking pan design of the Cuisinart bread maker makes it ideal for kitchens with limited counter space. Its compact footprint ensures that it won't take up too much room, yet it still has the capacity to produce generous loaves of bread.

Removable Components: Cleaning up after baking is a breeze thanks to the removable kneading paddle and bread pan. This makes it easy to wash these components thoroughly, ensuring that your bread maker stays clean and hygienic.

Monitoring Capabilities: The bread maker comes equipped with a lid that has a viewing window, allowing you to monitor the baking process without having to open the machine and disrupt the heat. Additionally, an interior light illuminates the bread as it bakes, giving you a clear view of its progress.

Versatility: While bread is the primary focus of this machine, it's capable of much more than just baking loaves. With its foolproof recipes and customizable settings, you can use it to make a variety of treats, including cakes, pizzas, jams, and sauces. This versatility makes it a valuable addition to any kitchen.

Healthy Options: If you're conscious of your dietary choices, the Cuisinart bread maker allows you to incorporate whole grains, nuts, and dried fruit into your recipes. This enables you to create healthier bread options that are packed with nutrients and flavor.

Delay-Start Timer: The 13-hour delay-start timer gives you the flexibility to start the baking process at a time that's convenient for you. Whether you want to wake up to the aroma of freshly baked bread in the morning or have a loaf ready and waiting for you when you get home from work, this feature allows you to plan ahead.

In summary, your Cuisinart compact automatic bread maker offers convenience, versatility, and customization options that empower you to explore the world of homemade bread and beyond. With its easy-to-use interface, compact design, and array of features, it's sure to become a staple in your kitchen arsenal.

Tips for Successful Bread Making with Cuisinart Machines

Making bread with a Cuisinart bread maker can be a delightful experience, yielding fresh, homemade loaves with minimal effort. To ensure success with your bread-making endeavors, consider the following tips tailored specifically for using Cuisinart machines:

Accurate Measurements: Precision is key when it comes to bread making. Ensure that you measure your ingredients accurately, especially flour. Use a kitchen

scale for best results, as measuring cups can vary in volume.

Use High-Quality Ingredients: The quality of your ingredients directly impacts the taste and texture of your bread. Opt for high-quality flour, fresh yeast, and filtered water. Fresh ingredients will yield the best results.

Follow the Instructions: Familiarize yourself with the user manual provided with your Cuisinart bread maker. Each model may have slightly different settings and instructions. Follow the recommended measurements, order of ingredients, and baking times for optimal results.

Experiment with Flours: While traditional bread recipes often call for all-purpose or bread flour, don't hesitate to experiment with different types of flour such as whole wheat, rye, or even gluten-free options. Keep in mind that different flours may require adjustments to the liquid content or rising time.

Check the Dough Consistency: Pay attention to the consistency of the dough during the kneading cycle. If the dough appears too dry and crumbly, add a tablespoon of water at a time until it forms a smooth, elastic ball. Conversely, if the dough is too wet and sticky, add a tablespoon of flour at a time until it reaches the desired consistency.

Customize Crust Preferences: Cuisinart bread makers offer multiple crust settings, allowing you to customize the crust color to your preference. Experiment with different settings to achieve the perfect crust – whether you prefer a light golden crust or a darker, more robust one.

Utilize Pre-Programmed Menu Options: Take advantage of the pre-programmed menu options available on your Cuisinart bread maker. These settings are designed to streamline the bread-making process for various types of bread, including basic white, whole wheat, gluten-free, and artisan loaves. Refer to the recipe book provided for specific instructions on each menu option.

Incorporate Add-Ins: Get creative with your bread by incorporating add-ins such as nuts, seeds, dried fruits, or herbs. Add these ingredients towards the end of the kneading cycle or as directed in your recipe to ensure even distribution throughout the dough.

Experiment with Recipes: While the recipe book provided with your Cuisinart bread maker offers a variety of foolproof recipes, don't be afraid to experiment with your own creations. Once you become familiar with the basic bread-making process, you can start experimenting with different ingredients, flavors, and techniques to create unique and delicious loaves.

Practice Patience: Bread making is a process that requires patience and practice. Don't be discouraged if your first few loaves don't turn out exactly as expected. Take note of any adjustments you make along the way and learn from each baking experience to improve your skills over time.

By following these tips and embracing the versatility of your Cuisinart bread maker, you can enjoy a wide range of delicious homemade breads tailored to your taste preferences. Whether you're a novice baker or a seasoned pro, the convenience and reliability of a Cuisinart machine make it easy to achieve bakery-quality results in the comfort of your own home.

What Is the Best Order to Put Ingredients in A Bread Machine?

When using a bread machine like the Cuisinart Compact Automatic Bread Maker, the order in which you add ingredients can significantly impact the outcome of your loaf. While most bread machines follow a similar sequence, it's always essential to consult your specific machine's manual for any nuances or requirements. Here's a breakdown of the typical order for adding ingredients:

Liquid Ingredients: Start by adding all your liquid ingredients to the bread pan. This includes water, milk, eggs, and any other liquids specified in your recipe. Adding liquids first helps to ensure that the dry ingredients are evenly distributed during mixing.

Dry Ingredients: Next, add your dry ingredients on top of the liquid. This

typically includes flour, sugar, salt, and any other dry ingredients like herbs, spices, or dried fruits. It's essential to measure your dry ingredients accurately, using the appropriate measuring cups for dry ingredients.

Yeast: Yeast is a crucial ingredient in bread making, as it is responsible for the rising of the dough. However, it's essential to keep it separate from the liquid until the mixing process begins. Make a small well or indentation in the center of your dry ingredients, and carefully add the yeast into this well. This prevents the yeast from activating too early and potentially affecting the rise of your bread.

Optional Ingredients: If your recipe calls for any additional ingredients such as nuts, seeds, chocolate chips, or dried fruits, these can be added on top of the dry ingredients. However, it's essential to ensure that these ingredients are evenly distributed throughout the dough to avoid uneven texture or pockets of ingredients.

Selecting the Program: Once all your ingredients are added to the bread pan, carefully place it into the bread machine and select the appropriate program for your recipe. Most bread machines offer a variety of pre-programmed settings for different types of bread, including basic white, whole wheat, gluten-free, and more. Choose the program that corresponds to your recipe for the best results.

Crust Shade and Loaf Size: Before starting the machine, you'll typically have the option to select the crust shade and loaf size according to your preferences. The Cuisinart Compact Automatic Bread Maker offers three crust shades: light, medium, or dark, and can bake up to a 2-pound loaf. Adjust these settings as desired before starting the machine.

Start the Machine: Once you've selected the program, crust shade, and loaf size, you can start the bread machine. Depending on the program you've chosen, the machine will begin mixing, kneading, rising, and baking the dough automatically. The process may take several hours, so it's essential to plan accordingly.

By following this recommended order for adding ingredients to your bread

machine, you can ensure that your loaf turns out consistently delicious, with the perfect texture and crust every time. Remember to consult your bread machine's manual and follow any specific instructions or guidelines provided by the manufacturer for the best results.

How to Store Your Bread?

Storing your freshly baked bread properly is crucial to maintaining its quality, freshness, and flavor. Here's a comprehensive guide on how to store your bread effectively:

Cooling Down: Allow your bread to cool completely before storing it. Placing warm bread in a storage container can create condensation, leading to a soggy crust and mold growth. Ideally, let the bread cool on a wire rack for at least an hour before storage.

Choosing the Right Container: The container you choose plays a significant role in preserving the quality of your bread. While some prefer using plastic bags, it's best to opt for containers that allow for airflow to prevent moisture buildup. Bread bins or paper bags with perforations are excellent choices as they maintain the bread's texture while preventing it from becoming too moist or too dry.

Wrapping Method: If you're using plastic bags, ensure the bread has cooled completely before wrapping it. Use plastic bags designed for bread storage or large, resealable plastic bags with some holes punched in for airflow. Avoid wrapping bread in plastic wrap alone, as it can trap moisture and lead to a soggy crust.

Paper Bags: Paper bags are a classic option for storing bread. They allow for airflow while protecting the bread from drying out too quickly. Place the bread in a paper bag and loosely fold the top to keep it covered. Make sure the bag is clean and dry before use to prevent contamination.

Bread Box: Investing in a bread box is a convenient and stylish way to store your bread. Bread boxes typically have ventilation holes or a wooden lid that helps

regulate moisture levels. Place your cooled bread inside the box and keep it in a cool, dry place away from direct sunlight.

Refrigeration: While refrigeration can help extend the shelf life of bread, it's not always the best option as it can cause the bread to dry out faster. If you live in a hot and humid climate or if you're not planning to consume the bread within a few days, refrigeration might be necessary. However, it's crucial to wrap the bread tightly in plastic wrap or aluminum foil to prevent it from absorbing odors and losing moisture.

Freezing: Freezing bread is an excellent way to preserve its freshness for an extended period. To freeze bread, slice it first and then wrap each slice individually in plastic wrap or aluminum foil. Place the wrapped slices in a freezer bag, removing as much air as possible before sealing. Frozen bread can be thawed at room temperature or warmed in the oven when ready to eat.

Avoid Moisture and Heat: Regardless of the storage method you choose, it's essential to keep your bread away from moisture and heat sources. Moisture

promotes mold growth, while heat accelerates staling. Store your bread in a cool, dry place away from the stove, dishwasher, or any other appliances that generate heat.

By following these tips, you can ensure that your freshly baked bread stays delicious and enjoyable for longer periods. Proper storage not only maintains the bread's quality but also enhances its flavor and texture over time.

Common Bread-Making Issues

Bread-making, despite its simplicity in concept, can sometimes present challenges even to seasoned bakers. Understanding common bread-making issues and their solutions can greatly enhance your baking experience with the Cuisinart Compact Automatic Bread Maker. Here are some common issues and how to address them:

Dense or Heavy Loaves:

Dense or heavy loaves often result from using too much flour or not enough liquid. Ensure that you measure ingredients accurately, especially flour, as too much can lead to a dense texture. Additionally, check the yeast's freshness and make sure it's properly activated during the initial mixing stage. Insufficient rising time or proofing can also lead to dense loaves. Ensure that the dough has doubled in size during the rising process before baking.

Sunken Top:

A sunken top can occur due to several reasons, including overproofing, using expired yeast, or too much liquid in the dough. Follow the recipe's proofing times carefully, as overproofing can cause the dough to collapse during baking. Ensure that your yeast is fresh and properly activated. Using too much liquid can also lead to a weak dough structure, causing the bread to collapse. Adjust the liquid

content accordingly based on the recipe and environmental conditions.

Uneven Rising:

Uneven rising can occur if the dough is not kneaded properly or if there are inconsistencies in temperature throughout the rising process. Ensure that the kneading paddle is properly attached and functioning during the kneading cycle. Additionally, try to maintain a consistent temperature in the environment where the dough is rising. Drafts or fluctuating temperatures can affect the dough's rising process. If possible, use a proofing box or warm oven to create a stable environment for rising.

Burnt Crust:

A burnt crust can result from baking at too high a temperature or for too long. Ensure that you select the appropriate crust shade setting based on your preference and monitor the baking process closely, especially towards the end. If you find that the crust is browning too quickly, you can tent it with aluminum foil to prevent further browning while allowing the bread to finish baking.

Gummy or Undercooked Interior:

An undercooked interior can result from several factors, including insufficient baking time, too much liquid in the dough, or using expired yeast. Ensure that you bake the bread for the full duration recommended in the recipe and that the internal temperature reaches the desired level, typically around 190-200°F (88-93°C). Adjust the liquid content if the dough appears too wet, as excess moisture can lead to a gummy texture. Always check the expiration date of your yeast and ensure it's properly activated during the mixing process.

Flat Loaves:

Flat loaves can occur if the dough is overproofed, the yeast is expired or not properly activated, or if the dough is too wet. Follow the recipe's proofing times carefully and ensure that the dough rises adequately but not excessively. Check the freshness and activation of the yeast before mixing the dough. Additionally, ensure that you measure ingredients accurately, especially flour, as too much can lead to a wetter dough and result in flat loaves.

Crumbly Texture:

A crumbly texture can result from using too much flour or not enough liquid, overmixing the dough, or insufficient kneading. Ensure that you measure ingredients accurately and follow the recipe's proportions carefully. Avoid overmixing the dough, as this can lead to a fragile gluten structure and a crumbly texture. Additionally, ensure that the dough is kneaded sufficiently to develop gluten, which provides structure and prevents the bread from becoming crumbly.

By understanding these common bread-making issues and their solutions, you can troubleshoot any problems that may arise and achieve consistently excellent results with your Cuisinart Compact Automatic Bread Maker. Remember to follow recipes carefully, measure ingredients accurately, and monitor the baking process closely to ensure success every time.

Chapter 1: Basic Breads

Rye Bread

Prep Time: 20 Minutes   Cook Time: 3 Hours 30 Minutes   Serves: 10

Ingredients:

- 1 1/3 cups warm water (110°F)
- 2 tablespoons molasses
- 2 tablespoons unsalted butter, softened
- 1 1/2 teaspoons salt
- 1 1/2 cups rye flour
- 2 cups bread flour
- 2 teaspoons caraway seeds
- 2 teaspoons active dry yeast

Directions:

1. Add the warm water, molasses, softened butter, and salt to the bread pan of your Cuisinart Bread Machine.
2. Sprinkle the rye flour and bread flour over the wet ingredients in the pan.
3. Add the caraway seeds on top of the flour mixture.
4. Create a small well in the center of the flour and add the active dry yeast into it.
5. Place the bread pan securely into the bread machine.
6. Choose the "Whole Wheat" program from the menu options.
7. Select your desired loaf size and crust color using the appropriate buttons.
8. Initiate the mixing, kneading, rising, and baking process by pressing the Start button.
9. If prompted by the paddle signal, consider removing the dough to reshape it before continuing.
10. Once the cycle finishes, carefully remove the bread pan from the machine and transfer the rye bread to a wire rack to cool.
11. Allow the bread to cool completely before slicing and serving.

Nutritional Value (Amount per Serving):

Calories: 182; Fat: 2.36; Carb: 34.94; Protein: 5.45

Oatmeal Bread

Prep Time: 20 Minutes   Cook Time: 3 Hours 30 Minutes   Serves: 12

Ingredients:

- 1 1/4 cups warm water (110°F)
- 2 tablespoons honey
- 2 tablespoons unsalted butter, softened

- 1 1/2 teaspoons salt
- 1 cup old-fashioned oats
- 3 cups bread flour
- 2 teaspoons active dry yeast

Directions:

1. In the bread pan of your Cuisinart Bread Machine, combine the warm water, honey, softened butter, and salt.
2. Add the old-fashioned oats on top of the wet ingredients in the pan.
3. Sprinkle the bread flour over the oats in the pan.
4. Create a small well in the center of the flour and add the active dry yeast into it.
5. Place the bread pan securely into the bread machine.
6. Choose the "White" program from the menu options.
7. Select your desired loaf size and crust color using the appropriate buttons.
8. Initiate the mixing, kneading, rising, and baking process by pressing the Start button.
9. If prompted by the paddle signal, consider removing the dough to reshape it before continuing.
10. Once the cycle finishes, carefully remove the bread pan from the machine and transfer the oatmeal bread to a wire rack to cool.
11. Allow the bread to cool completely before slicing and serving.

Nutritional Value (Amount per Serving):

Calories: 167; Fat: 2.46; Carb: 33.19; Protein: 5.82

Potato Bread

Prep Time: 30 Minutes   Cook Time: 3 Hours 45 Minutes   Serves: 10

Ingredients:

- 3/4 cup warm water (110°F)
- 1/2 cup mashed potatoes, cooled
- 2 tablespoons unsalted butter, softened
- 2 tablespoons granulated sugar
- 1 1/2 teaspoons salt
- 3 1/2 cups bread flour
- 2 teaspoons active dry yeast

Directions:

1. Add the warm water, mashed potatoes, softened butter, granulated sugar, and salt to the bread pan of your Cuisinart Bread Machine.
2. Sprinkle the bread flour over the wet ingredients in the pan.
3. Create a small well in the center of the flour and add the active dry yeast into it.
4. Place the bread pan securely into the bread machine.
5. Choose the "White" program from the menu options.

6. Select your desired loaf size and crust color using the appropriate buttons.
7. Initiate the mixing, kneading, rising, and baking process by pressing the Start button.
8. If prompted by the paddle signal, consider removing the dough to reshape it before continuing.
9. Once the cycle finishes, carefully remove the bread pan from the machine and transfer the potato bread to a wire rack to cool.
10. Allow the bread to cool completely before slicing and serving.

Nutritional Value (Amount per Serving):

Calories: 202; Fat: 2.41; Carb: 38.01; Protein: 6.31

Cinnamon Raisin Bread

Prep Time: 25 Minutes   Cook Time: 3 Hours 30 Minutes   Serves: 12

Ingredients:

- 1 cup warm water (110°F)
- 2 tablespoons unsalted butter, softened
- 1/4 cup honey
- 1 teaspoon salt
- 3 cups bread flour
- 2 teaspoons ground cinnamon
- 1 cup raisins
- 2 teaspoons active dry yeast

Directions:

1. In the bread pan of your Cuisinart Bread Machine, combine the warm water, softened butter, honey, and salt.
2. Sprinkle the bread flour over the wet ingredients in the pan.
3. Add the ground cinnamon on top of the flour.
4. Scatter the raisins over the flour mixture.
5. Create a small well in the center of the flour and add the active dry yeast into it.
6. Place the bread pan securely into the bread machine.
7. Choose the "Sweet" program from the menu options.
8. Select your desired loaf size and crust color using the appropriate buttons.
9. Initiate the mixing, kneading, rising, and baking process by pressing the Start button.
10. If prompted by the paddle signal, consider removing the dough to reshape it before continuing.
11. Once the cycle finishes, carefully remove the bread pan from the machine and transfer the cinnamon raisin bread to a wire rack to cool.
12. Allow the bread to cool completely before slicing and serving.

Nutritional Value (Amount per Serving):

Calories: 160; Fat: 1.91; Carb: 31.32; Protein: 4.49

Honey Wheat Bread

Prep Time: 20 Minutes   Cook Time: 3 Hours 30 Minutes   Serves: 12

Ingredients:

- 1 1/4 cups warm water (110°F)
- 2 tablespoons honey
- 2 tablespoons unsalted butter, softened
- 1 1/2 teaspoons salt
- 1 1/2 cups whole wheat flour
- 1 1/2 cups bread flour
- 2 teaspoons active dry yeast

Directions:

1. In the bread pan of your Cuisinart Bread Machine, combine the warm water, honey, softened butter, and salt.
2. Add the whole wheat flour and bread flour on top of the wet ingredients in the pan.
3. Create a small well in the center of the flour and add the active dry yeast into it.
4. Place the bread pan securely into the bread machine.
5. Choose the "Whole Wheat" program from the menu options.
6. Select your desired loaf size and crust color using the appropriate buttons.
7. Initiate the mixing, kneading, rising, and baking process by pressing the Start button.
8. If prompted by the paddle signal, consider removing the dough to reshape it before continuing.
9. Once the cycle finishes, carefully remove the bread pan from the machine and transfer the honey wheat bread to a wire rack to cool.
10. Allow the bread to cool completely before slicing and serving.

Nutritional Value (Amount per Serving):

Calories: 137; Fat: 2; Carb: 26.38; Protein: 4.39

Cornbread

Prep Time: 15 Minutes   Cook Time: 3 Hours 15 Minutes   Serves: 10

Ingredients:

- 1 cup cornmeal
- 1 cup all-purpose flour
- 2 tablespoons granulated sugar
- 1 teaspoon salt
- 1 teaspoon baking powder
- 1/2 teaspoon baking soda
- 1 1/4 cups buttermilk
- 1/4 cup unsalted butter, melted
- 2 eggs

Directions:

1. In a large mixing bowl, combine the cornmeal, all-purpose flour, sugar,

salt, baking powder, and baking soda.

2. In a separate bowl, whisk together the buttermilk, melted butter, and eggs.
3. Pour the wet ingredients into the dry ingredients and stir until just combined.
4. Choose the "Bake" program and select your desired loaf size and crust color using the appropriate buttons.
5. Grease the bread pan with butter or cooking spray.
6. Pour the cornbread batter into the bread pan.
7. Place the bread pan into the bread machine and close the lid.
8. Press Start to begin the baking process.
9. Once the cycle is complete, carefully remove the bread pan from the machine and allow the cornbread to cool for a few minutes before slicing and serving.

Nutritional Value (Amount per Serving):

Calories: 176; Fat: 5.68; Carb: 25.51; Protein: 5.4

Sunflower Seed Bread

Prep Time: 20 Minutes   Cook Time: 3 Hours 30 Minutes   Serves: 12

Ingredients:

- 1 1/4 cups warm water (110°F)
- 2 tablespoons honey
- 2 tablespoons unsalted butter, softened
- 1 1/2 teaspoons salt
- 3 cups bread flour
- 1/2 cup sunflower seeds
- 2 teaspoons active dry yeast

Directions:

1. In the bread pan of your Cuisinart Bread Machine, combine the warm water, honey, softened butter, and salt.
2. Add the bread flour on top of the wet ingredients in the pan.
3. Sprinkle the sunflower seeds over the flour.
4. Create a small well in the center of the flour and add the active dry yeast into it.
5. Place the bread pan securely into the bread machine.
6. Choose the "White" program from the menu options.
7. Select your desired loaf size and crust color using the appropriate buttons.
8. Initiate the mixing, kneading, rising, and baking process by pressing the Start button.
9. If prompted by the paddle signal, consider removing the dough to reshape it before continuing.
10. Once the cycle finishes, carefully remove the bread pan from the machine and transfer the sunflower seed bread to a wire rack to cool.

11. Allow the bread to cool completely before slicing and serving.

Nutritional Value (Amount per Serving):

Calories:182 ; Fat: 4.91; Carb: 29.17; Protein: 5.67

Rosemary Olive Oil Bread

Prep Time: 20 Minutes   Cook Time: 3 Hours 30 Minutes   Serves: 12

Ingredients:

- 1 1/4 cups warm water (110°F)
- 2 tablespoons olive oil
- 1 tablespoon honey
- 1 1/2 teaspoons salt
- 3 1/2 cups bread flour
- 2 teaspoons dried rosemary
- 1/2 cup pitted and chopped Kalamata olives
- 2 teaspoons active dry yeast

Directions:

1. Add the warm water, olive oil, honey, and salt to the bread pan of your Cuisinart Bread Machine.
2. Sprinkle the bread flour over the liquid ingredients in the pan.
3. Add the dried rosemary and chopped olives on top of the flour.
4. Create a small well in the center of the flour and add the active dry yeast into it.
5. Place the bread pan securely into the bread machine.
6. Choose the "White" program from the menu options.
7. Select your desired loaf size and crust color using the appropriate buttons.
8. Initiate the mixing, kneading, rising, and baking process by pressing the Start button.
9. If prompted by the paddle signal, consider removing the dough to reshape it before continuing.
10. Once the cycle finishes, carefully remove the bread pan from the machine and transfer the rosemary olive oil bread to a wire rack to cool.
11. Allow the bread to cool completely before slicing and serving.

Nutritional Value (Amount per Serving):

Calories: 178; Fat: 3.57; Carb: 31.07; Protein: 5.11

Jalapeno Cornbread

Prep Time: 15 Minutes   Cook Time: 3 Hours 15 Minutes   Serves: 10

Ingredients:

- 1 cup cornmeal
- 1 cup all-purpose flour

- 2 tablespoons granulated sugar
- 1 teaspoon salt
- 1 teaspoon baking powder
- 1/2 teaspoon baking soda
- 1 1/4 cups buttermilk
- 1/4 cup unsalted butter, melted
- 2 eggs
- 1/2 cup canned diced jalapenos, drained

Directions:

1. In a large mixing bowl, combine the cornmeal, all-purpose flour, sugar, salt, baking powder, and baking soda.
2. In a separate bowl, whisk together the buttermilk, melted butter, and eggs.
3. Pour the wet ingredients into the dry ingredients and stir until just combined.
4. Fold in the diced jalapenos until evenly distributed throughout the batter.
5. Select "Bake" setting and grease the bread pan with butter or cooking spray.
6. Pour the jalapeno cornbread batter into the prepared bread pan.
7. Place the bread pan into the bread machine and close the lid.
8. Press Start to begin the baking process.
9. Once the cycle is complete, carefully remove the bread pan from the machine and allow the cornbread to cool for a few minutes before slicing and serving.

Nutritional Value (Amount per Serving):

Calories: 178; Fat: 5.7; Carb: 25.81; Protein: 5.44

Pumpernickel Bread

Prep Time: 25 Minutes   Cook Time: 3 Hours 45 Minutes   Serves: 12

Ingredients:

- 1 1/4 cups warm water (110°F)
- 2 tablespoons molasses
- 2 tablespoons unsalted butter, softened
- 1 1/2 teaspoons salt
- 1 cup rye flour
- 2 1/2 cups bread flour
- 2 tablespoons cocoa powder
- 2 teaspoons caraway seeds
- 2 teaspoons active dry yeast

Directions:

1. In the bread pan of your Cuisinart Bread Machine, combine the warm water, molasses, softened butter, and salt.
2. Add the rye flour and bread flour on top of the wet ingredients in the pan.
3. Sprinkle the cocoa powder and caraway seeds over the flour.
4. Create a small well in the center of the flour and add the active dry yeast into it.
5. Place the bread pan securely into the bread machine.

6. Choose the "Whole Wheat" program from the menu options.
7. Select your desired loaf size and crust color using the appropriate buttons.
8. Initiate the mixing, kneading, rising, and baking process by pressing the Start button.
9. If prompted by the paddle signal, consider removing the dough to reshape it before continuing.
10. Once the cycle finishes, carefully remove the bread pan from the machine and transfer the pumpernickel bread to a wire rack to cool.
11. Allow the bread to cool completely before slicing and serving.

Nutritional Value (Amount per Serving):

Calories: 159; Fat: 2.11; Carb: 30.58; Protein: 4.92

Jalapeño Cheddar Bread

Prep Time: 25 Minutes   Cook Time: 3 Hours 30 Minutes   Serves: 12

Ingredients:

- 1 1/4 cups warm water (110°F)
- 2 tablespoons unsalted butter, softened
- 1 tablespoon granulated sugar
- 1 1/2 teaspoons salt
- 3 1/2 cups bread flour
- 1 cup shredded cheddar cheese
- 2-3 jalapeños, seeded and finely diced
- 2 teaspoons active dry yeast

Directions:

1. In the bread pan of your Cuisinart Bread Machine, combine the warm water, softened butter, sugar, and salt.
2. Add the bread flour on top of the wet ingredients in the pan.
3. Sprinkle the shredded cheddar cheese and diced jalapeños over the flour.
4. Create a small well in the center of the flour and add the active dry yeast into it.
5. Place the bread pan securely into the bread machine.
6. Choose the "White" program from the menu options.
7. Select your desired loaf size and crust color using the appropriate buttons.
8. Initiate the mixing, kneading, rising, and baking process by pressing the Start button.
9. If prompted by the paddle signal, consider removing the dough to reshape it before continuing.
10. Once the cycle finishes, carefully remove the bread pan from the machine and transfer the jalapeño cheddar bread to a wire rack to cool.
11. Allow the bread to cool completely before slicing and serving.

Nutritional Value (Amount per Serving):

Calories: 228; Fat: 6.72; Carb: 33.13; Protein: 8.9

Chapter 2: Sourdough Breads

Classic Sourdough Loaf

Prep Time: 15 Minutes   Cook Time: 3 Hours   Serves: 12

Ingredients:

- 1 cup active sourdough starter
- 1 1/4 cups lukewarm water
- 4 cups bread flour
- 2 teaspoons salt

Directions:

1. Place the sourdough starter, lukewarm water, bread flour, and salt into the bread machine pan in the order listed.
2. Select the "Artisan Dough" program and desired loaf size and crust shade (light, medium, or dark).
3. Press Start to begin the cycle.
4. Once the cycle is complete, carefully remove the loaf from the bread machine and allow it to cool on a wire rack before slicing.

Nutritional Value (Amount per Serving):

Calories: 217; Fat: 1.98; Carb: 39.72; Protein: 11.94

Sourdough Rye Bread

Prep Time: 15 Minutes   Cook Time: 3 Hours 30 Minutes   Serves: 10

Ingredients:

- 1 cup active sourdough starter
- 1 1/4 cups lukewarm water
- 2 cups bread flour
- 1 cup rye flour
- 1 tablespoon caraway seeds (optional)
- 2 teaspoons salt

Directions:

1. Add the sourdough starter, lukewarm water, bread flour, rye flour, caraway seeds (if using), and salt to the bread machine pan in the order listed.
2. Select the "Whole Wheat" program and desired loaf size and crust shade.
3. Press Start to begin the cycle.
4. After the cycle is complete, remove the bread from the machine and let it cool on a wire rack before slicing.

Nutritional Value (Amount per Serving):

Calories: 199; Fat: 2.17; Carb: 35.82; Protein: 12.29

Sourdough Olive Bread

Prep Time: 15 Minutes   Cook Time: 3 Hours 15 Minutes   Serves: 8

Ingredients:

- 1 cup active sourdough starter
- 1 cup lukewarm water
- 3 1/2 cups bread flour
- 1 teaspoon salt
- 1/2 cup pitted and chopped Kalamata olives
- 2 tablespoons chopped fresh rosemary

Directions:

1. Place the sourdough starter, lukewarm water, bread flour, salt, chopped olives, and rosemary into the bread machine pan in the order listed.
2. Select the "French" program and desired loaf size and crust shade.
3. Press Start to begin the cycle.
4. Once the cycle is complete, remove the bread from the machine and cool it on a wire rack before slicing.

Nutritional Value (Amount per Serving):

Calories: 305; Fat: 3.74; Carb: 53.98; Protein: 16.97

Sourdough Walnut Bread

Prep Time: 15 Minutes   Cook Time: 3 Hours 30 Minutes   Serves: 10

Ingredients:

- 1 cup active sourdough starter
- 1 1/4 cups lukewarm water
- 3 1/2 cups bread flour
- 1 teaspoon salt
- 1/2 cup chopped walnuts

Directions:

1. Add the sourdough starter, lukewarm water, bread flour, salt, and chopped walnuts to the bread machine pan in the order listed.
2. Select the "Whole Wheat" program and desired loaf size and crust shade.
3. Press Start to begin the cycle.
4. After baking is complete, remove the bread from the machine and let it cool on a wire rack before slicing.

Nutritional Value (Amount per Serving):

Calories: 262; Fat: 4.87; Carb: 43.24; Protein: 14.12

Sourdough Cinnamon Raisin Bread

Prep Time: 15 Minutes   Cook Time: 3 Hours   Serves: 12

Ingredients:

- 1 cup active sourdough starter
- 1 1/4 cups lukewarm water

- 3 1/2 cups bread flour
- 1/4 cup sugar
- 1 teaspoon cinnamon
- 1 teaspoon salt
- 1/2 cup raisins

Directions:

1. Place the sourdough starter, lukewarm water, bread flour, sugar, cinnamon, salt, and raisins into the bread machine pan in the order listed.
2. Select the "Sweet" program and desired loaf size and crust shade.
3. Press Start to begin the cycle.
4. When the bread is done, remove it from the machine and let it cool on a wire rack before slicing and serving.

Nutritional Value (Amount per Serving):

Calories: 205; Fat: 1.88; Carb: 37.85; Protein: 11.27

Sourdough Multigrain Bread

Prep Time: 15 Minutes   Cook Time: 3 Hours 30 Minutes   Serves: 10

Ingredients:

- 1 cup active sourdough starter
- 1 1/4 cups lukewarm water
- 2 1/2 cups bread flour
- 1 cup multigrain cereal blend (such as oats, flaxseed, and millet)
- 1/4 cup honey
- 2 teaspoons salt

Directions:

1. Add the sourdough starter, lukewarm water, bread flour, multigrain cereal blend, honey, and salt to the bread machine pan in the order listed.
2. Select the "Whole Wheat" program and desired loaf size and crust shade.
3. Press Start to begin the cycle.
4. After baking is complete, remove the bread from the machine and let it cool on a wire rack before slicing.

Nutritional Value (Amount per Serving):

Calories: 222; Fat: 2.05; Carb: 42.48; Protein: 12

Sourdough Garlic and Herb Bread

Prep Time: 15 Minutes   Cook Time: 3 Hours 15 Minutes   Serves: 8

Ingredients:

- 1 cup active sourdough starter

- 1 1/4 cups lukewarm water
- 3 1/2 cups bread flour
- 2 teaspoons salt
- 2 cloves garlic, minced
- 2 tablespoons chopped fresh herbs (such as rosemary, thyme, and parsley)

Directions:

1. Place the sourdough starter, lukewarm water, bread flour, salt, minced garlic, and chopped herbs into the bread machine pan in the order listed.
2. Select the "Artisan Dough" program and desired loaf size and crust shade.
3. Press Start to begin the cycle.
4. Once the cycle is complete, remove the bread from the machine and cool it on a wire rack before slicing.

Nutritional Value (Amount per Serving):

Calories: 297; Fat: 2.83; Carb: 54.04; Protein: 16.95

Sourdough Sun-Dried Tomato and Basil Bread

Prep Time: 15 Minutes   Cook Time: 3 Hours 15 Minutes   Serves: 8

Ingredients:

- 1 cup active sourdough starter
- 1 cup lukewarm water
- 3 1/2 cups bread flour
- 2 teaspoons salt
- 1/2 cup chopped sun-dried tomatoes (packed in oil)
- 2 tablespoons chopped fresh basil

Directions:

1. Add the sourdough starter, lukewarm water, bread flour, salt, chopped sun-dried tomatoes, and chopped basil to the bread machine pan in the order listed.
2. Select the "French" program and desired loaf size and crust shade.
3. Press Start to begin the cycle.
4. After baking is complete, remove the bread from the machine and let it cool on a wire rack before slicing.

Nutritional Value (Amount per Serving):

Calories: 303; Fat: 2.93; Carb: 55.26; Protein: 17.38

Sourdough Cranberry Walnut Bread

Prep Time: 15 Minutes   Cook Time: 3 Hours   Serves: 12

Ingredients:

- 1 cup active sourdough starter
- 1 1/4 cups lukewarm water
- 3 1/2 cups bread flour

- 1 teaspoon salt
- 1/2 cup dried cranberries
- 1/2 cup chopped walnuts

Directions:

1. Place the sourdough starter, lukewarm water, bread flour, salt, dried cranberries, and chopped walnuts into the bread machine pan in the order listed.
2. Select the "Sweet" program and desired loaf size and crust shade.
3. Press Start to begin the cycle.
4. When the bread is done, remove it from the machine and let it cool on a wire rack before slicing and serving.

Nutritional Value (Amount per Serving):

Calories: 224; Fat: 4.07; Carb: 37.46; Protein: 11.77

Sourdough Asiago Cheese Bread

Prep Time: 15 Minutes   Cook Time: 3 Hours   Serves: 12

Ingredients:

- 1 cup active sourdough starter
- 1 1/4 cups lukewarm water
- 3 1/2 cups bread flour

- 1 teaspoon salt
- 1 cup grated Asiago cheese

Directions:

1. Add the sourdough starter, lukewarm water, bread flour, salt, and grated Asiago cheese to the bread machine pan in the order listed.
2. Select the "French" program and desired loaf size and crust shade.
3. Press Start to begin the cycle.
4. After baking is complete, remove the bread from the machine and let it cool on a wire rack before slicing.

Nutritional Value (Amount per Serving):

Calories: 237; Fat: 5.21; Carb: 35.65; Protein: 13.95

Sourdough Seeded Bread

Prep Time: 15 Minutes   Cook Time: 3 Hours 30 Minutes   Serves: 10

Ingredients:

- 1 cup active sourdough starter

- 1 1/4 cups lukewarm water
- 3 1/2 cups bread flour
- 1 teaspoon salt
- 1/4 cup mixed seeds (such as sesame seeds, poppy seeds, and pumpkin seeds)

Directions:

1. Place the sourdough starter, lukewarm water, bread flour, salt, and mixed seeds into the bread machine pan in the order listed.
2. Select the "Whole Wheat" program and desired loaf size and crust shade.
3. Press Start to begin the cycle.
4. Once the bread is done, remove it from the machine and let it cool on a wire rack before slicing.

Nutritional Value (Amount per Serving):

Calories: 259; Fat: 4.55; Carb: 43.13; Protein: 14.28

Sourdough Herb Bread

Prep Time: 15 Minutes   Cook Time: 3 Hours 15 Minutes   Serves: 8

Ingredients:

- 1 cup active sourdough starter
- 1 cup lukewarm water
- 3 1/2 cups bread flour
- 1 teaspoon salt
- 2 tablespoons chopped fresh herbs (such as rosemary, thyme, and parsley)

Directions:

1. Add the sourdough starter, lukewarm water, bread flour, salt, and chopped fresh herbs to the bread machine pan in the order listed.
2. Select the "French" program and desired loaf size and crust shade.
3. Press Start to begin the cycle.
4. Once the bread is baked, remove it from the machine and let it cool on a wire rack before slicing.

Nutritional Value (Amount per Serving):

Calories: 296; Fat: 2.83; Carb: 53.79; Protein: 16.9

Sourdough Pumpernickel Bread

Prep Time: 15 Minutes   Cook Time: 3 Hours 30 Minutes   Serves: 10

Ingredients:

- 1 cup active sourdough starter
- 1 1/4 cups lukewarm water

- 2 cups bread flour
- 1 cup rye flour
- 1/4 cup molasses
- 2 tablespoons cocoa powder
- 2 teaspoons instant coffee granules
- 2 teaspoons caraway seeds
- 1 1/2 teaspoons salt

Directions:

1. Place the sourdough starter, lukewarm water, bread flour, rye flour, molasses, cocoa powder, instant coffee granules, caraway seeds, and salt into the bread machine pan in the order listed.
2. Select the "Whole Wheat" program and desired loaf size and crust shade.
3. Press Start to begin the cycle.
4. After baking is complete, remove the bread from the machine and let it cool on a wire rack before slicing.

Nutritional Value (Amount per Serving):

Calories: 225; Fat: 2.28; Carb: 42.62; Protein: 12.44

Sourdough Asiago and Black Pepper Bread

Prep Time: 15 Minutes   Cook Time: 3 Hours 15 Minutes   Serves: 8

Ingredients:

- 1 cup active sourdough starter
- 1 cup lukewarm water
- 3 1/2 cups bread flour
- 1 teaspoon salt
- 1 cup shredded Asiago cheese
- 1 tablespoon coarsely ground black pepper

Directions:

1. Add the sourdough starter, lukewarm water, bread flour, salt, shredded Asiago cheese, and coarsely ground black pepper to the bread machine pan in the order listed.
2. Select the "Artisan Dough" program and desired loaf size and crust shade.
3. Press Start to begin the cycle.
4. Once the bread is done, remove it from the machine and let it cool on a wire rack before slicing.

Nutritional Value (Amount per Serving):

Calories: 351; Fat: 6.6; Carb: 55.1; Protein: 20.75

Chapter 3: Fruit Breads

Pineapple Coconut Bread

Prep Time: 15 Minutes   Cook Time: 3 Hours   Serves: 10

Ingredients:

- 1/2 cup canned pineapple chunks, drained and chopped
- 1/4 cup shredded coconut
- 1/4 cup unsalted butter, melted
- 2 large eggs
- 1/2 cup granulated sugar
- 1 teaspoon vanilla extract
- 2 cups all-purpose flour
- 1 1/2 teaspoons baking powder
- 1/2 teaspoon baking soda
- 1/4 teaspoon salt

Directions:

1. In a mixing bowl, combine chopped pineapple chunks, shredded coconut, melted butter, eggs, sugar, and vanilla extract.
2. In a separate bowl, sift together all-purpose flour, baking powder, baking soda, and salt.
3. Gradually add the dry ingredients to the wet ingredients, stirring until just combined.
4. Pour the batter into the bread machine pan.
5. Select the "Sweet" program and the desired loaf size and crust shade.
6. Press Start to begin the baking cycle.
7. Once the cycle is complete, carefully remove the bread from the machine and let it cool on a wire rack before slicing.

Nutritional Value (Amount per Serving):

Calories: 163; Fat: 4.26; Carb: 27.54; Protein: 3.4

Raspberry Chocolate Chip Bread

Prep Time: 15 Minutes   Cook Time: 3 Hours   Serves: 10

Ingredients:

- 1/2 cup milk
- 1/4 cup unsalted butter, melted
- 2 large eggs
- 1 teaspoon vanilla extract
- 2 cups all-purpose flour
- 1/2 cup granulated sugar
- 1 1/2 teaspoons baking powder
- 1/2 teaspoon baking soda
- 1/4 teaspoon salt
- 1 cup fresh raspberries
- 1/2 cup semisweet chocolate chips

Directions:

1. In a mixing bowl, whisk together milk, melted butter, eggs, and vanilla extract until well combined.
2. In a separate bowl, sift together all-purpose flour, sugar, baking powder, baking soda, and salt.
3. Gradually add the dry ingredients to the wet ingredients, stirring until just combined.
4. Gently fold in the fresh raspberries and semisweet chocolate chips.
5. Pour the batter into the bread machine pan.
6. Select the "Sweet" program and the desired loaf size and crust shade.
7. Press Start to begin the baking cycle.
8. Once the cycle is complete, carefully remove the bread from the machine and let it cool on a wire rack before slicing.

Nutritional Value (Amount per Serving):

Calories: 241; Fat: 7.63; Carb: 38.64; Protein: 4.41

Pear Ginger Bread

Prep Time: 15 Minutes   Cook Time: 3 Hours   Serves: 10

Ingredients:

- 1/2 cup diced ripe pear
- 1/4 cup chopped crystallized ginger
- 1/4 cup unsalted butter, softened
- 2 tablespoons honey
- 1/2 cup buttermilk
- 2 large eggs
- 2 cups all-purpose flour
- 1 teaspoon baking powder
- 1/2 teaspoon baking soda
- 1/4 teaspoon salt
- 1/2 teaspoon ground ginger
- 1/4 teaspoon ground cinnamon

Directions:

1. In a mixing bowl, combine diced pear, chopped crystallized ginger, softened butter, honey, buttermilk, and eggs.
2. In a separate bowl, sift together all-purpose flour, baking powder, baking soda, salt, ground ginger, and ground cinnamon.
3. Gradually add the dry ingredients to the wet ingredients, stirring until just combined.
4. Pour the batter into the bread machine pan.
5. Select the "Sweet" program and the desired loaf size and crust shade.
6. Press Start to begin the baking cycle.
7. Once the cycle is complete, carefully remove the bread from the machine and let it cool on a wire rack before slicing.

Nutritional Value (Amount per Serving):

Calories: 160; Fat: 4.38; Carb: 26.58; Protein: 3.81

Peach Pecan Bread

Prep Time: 15 Minutes   Cook Time: 3 Hours   Serves: 10

Ingredients:

- 1/2 cup canned peaches, drained and chopped
- 1/4 cup chopped pecans
- 1/4 cup unsalted butter, melted
- 2 large eggs
- 1/2 cup granulated sugar
- 1 teaspoon vanilla extract
- 2 cups all-purpose flour
- 1 1/2 teaspoons baking powder
- 1/2 teaspoon baking soda
- 1/4 teaspoon salt

Directions:

1. In a mixing bowl, combine chopped peaches, chopped pecans, melted butter, eggs, sugar, and vanilla extract.
2. In a separate bowl, sift together all-purpose flour, baking powder, baking soda, and salt.
3. Gradually add the dry ingredients to the wet ingredients, stirring until just combined.
4. Pour the batter into the bread machine pan.
5. Select the "Sweet" program and the desired loaf size and crust shade.
6. Press Start to begin the baking cycle.
7. Once the cycle is complete, carefully remove the bread from the machine and let it cool on a wire rack before slicing.

Nutritional Value (Amount per Serving):

Calories: 178; Fat: 6.03; Carb: 27.55; Protein: 3.59

Fig Walnut Bread

Prep Time: 15 Minutes   Cook Time: 3 Hours   Serves: 10

Ingredients:

- 1/2 cup chopped dried figs
- 1/4 cup chopped walnuts
- 1/4 cup unsalted butter, softened
- 2 tablespoons honey
- 1/2 cup milk
- 2 large eggs
- 2 cups bread flour
- 1 teaspoon salt
- 1 teaspoon ground cinnamon

Directions:

1. In the bread machine pan, combine chopped dried figs, chopped walnuts, softened butter, honey, milk, and eggs.
2. Add bread flour, salt, and ground cinnamon to the pan.
3. Make a small well in the center of the flour mixture and add the yeast.

4. Select the "Sweet" program and the desired loaf size and crust shade.
5. Press Start to begin the baking cycle.
6. Once the cycle is complete, carefully remove the bread from the machine and let it cool on a wire rack before slicing.

Nutritional Value (Amount per Serving):

Calories: 190; Fat: 6.22; Carb: 29.28; Protein: 4.96

Plum Streusel Bread

Prep Time: 15 Minutes   Cook Time: 3 Hours   Serves: 10

Ingredients:

- 1/2 cup chopped fresh plums
- 1/4 cup unsalted butter, melted
- 1/2 cup granulated sugar
- 2 large eggs
- 1 teaspoon vanilla extract
- 2 cups all-purpose flour
- 1 1/2 teaspoons baking powder
- 1/2 teaspoon baking soda
- 1/4 teaspoon salt
- 1/4 cup all-purpose flour
- 2 tablespoons granulated sugar
- 2 tablespoons unsalted butter, cold

Directions:

1. In a mixing bowl, combine chopped fresh plums, melted butter, sugar, eggs, and vanilla extract.
2. In a separate bowl, sift together all-purpose flour, baking powder, baking soda, and salt.
3. Gradually add the dry ingredients to the wet ingredients, stirring until just combined.
4. Pour the batter into the bread machine pan.
5. In a small bowl, combine flour and sugar. Cut in cold butter until crumbly. Sprinkle over the batter in the pan.
6. Select the "Bake" program and the desired loaf size and crust shade.
7. Press Start to begin the baking cycle.
8. Once the cycle is complete, carefully remove the bread from the machine and let it cool on a wire rack before slicing.

Nutritional Value (Amount per Serving):

Calories: 194; Fat: 5.82; Carb: 31.58; Protein: 3.77

Mixed Berry Bread

Prep Time: 15 Minutes   Cook Time: 3 Hours   Serves: 10

Ingredients:

- 1/2 cup mixed berries (such as strawberries, blueberries, and raspberries), chopped
- 1/4 cup unsalted butter, melted
- 1/2 cup granulated sugar
- 2 large eggs
- 1 teaspoon vanilla extract
- 2 cups all-purpose flour
- 1 1/2 teaspoons baking powder
- 1/2 teaspoon baking soda
- 1/4 teaspoon salt

Directions:

1. In a mixing bowl, combine chopped mixed berries, melted butter, sugar, eggs, and vanilla extract.
2. In a separate bowl, sift together all-purpose flour, baking powder, baking soda, and salt.
3. Gradually add the dry ingredients to the wet ingredients, stirring until just combined.
4. Pour the batter into the bread machine pan.
5. Select the "Bake" program and the desired loaf size and crust shade.
6. Press Start to begin the baking cycle.
7. Once the cycle is complete, carefully remove the bread from the machine and let it cool on a wire rack before slicing.

Nutritional Value (Amount per Serving):

Calories: 156; Fat: 4.25; Carb: 25.96; Protein: 3.36

Mango Coconut Bread

Prep Time: 15 Minutes   Cook Time: 3 Hours   Serves: 10

Ingredients:

- 1/2 cup diced ripe mango
- 1/4 cup shredded coconut
- 1/4 cup unsalted butter, softened
- 2 tablespoons honey
- 1/2 cup coconut milk
- 2 large eggs
- 2 cups bread flour
- 1 teaspoon salt
- 1/2 teaspoon ground ginger

Directions:

1. In the bread machine pan, combine diced mango, shredded coconut, softened butter, honey, coconut milk, and eggs.
2. Add bread flour, salt, and ground ginger to the pan.
3. Make a small well in the center of the flour mixture and add the yeast.

4. Select the "Sweet" program and the desired loaf size and crust shade.
5. Press Start to begin the baking cycle.
6. Once the cycle is complete, carefully remove the bread from the machine and let it cool on a wire rack before slicing.

Nutritional Value (Amount per Serving):

Calories: 185; Fat: 7.35; Carb: 25.64; Protein: 4.41

Blackberry Basil Bread

Prep Time: 15 Minutes   Cook Time: 3 Hours   Serves: 10

Ingredients:

- 1/2 cup fresh blackberries, chopped
- 2 tablespoons fresh basil leaves, finely chopped
- 1/4 cup unsalted butter, melted
- 1/2 cup granulated sugar
- 2 large eggs
- 1 teaspoon vanilla extract
- 2 cups all-purpose flour
- 1 1/2 teaspoons baking powder
- 1/2 teaspoon baking soda
- 1/4 teaspoon salt

Directions:

1. In a mixing bowl, combine chopped fresh blackberries, finely chopped basil leaves, melted butter, sugar, eggs, and vanilla extract.
2. In a separate bowl, sift together all-purpose flour, baking powder, baking soda, and salt.
3. Gradually add the dry ingredients to the wet ingredients, stirring until just combined.
4. Pour the batter into the bread machine pan.
5. Select the "Bake" program and the desired loaf size and crust shade.
6. Press Start to begin the baking cycle.
7. Once the cycle is complete, carefully remove the bread from the machine and let it cool on a wire rack before slicing.

Nutritional Value (Amount per Serving):

Calories: 163; Fat: 4.25; Carb: 27.55; Protein: 3.48

Kiwi Lime Bread

Prep Time: 15 Minutes   Cook Time: 3 Hours   Serves: 10

Ingredients:

- 1/2 cup diced kiwi
- Zest of 2 limes
- 1/4 cup unsalted butter, softened
- 1/2 cup granulated sugar
- 2 large eggs
- 1 teaspoon vanilla extract
- 2 cups all-purpose flour
- 1 1/2 teaspoons baking powder
- 1/2 teaspoon baking soda
- 1/4 teaspoon salt

Directions:

1. In a mixing bowl, combine diced kiwi, lime zest, softened butter, sugar, eggs, and vanilla extract.
2. In a separate bowl, sift together all-purpose flour, baking powder, baking soda, and salt.
3. Gradually add the dry ingredients to the wet ingredients, stirring until just combined.
4. Pour the batter into the bread machine pan.
5. Select the "Bake" program and the desired loaf size and crust shade.
6. Press Start to begin the baking cycle.
7. Once the cycle is complete, carefully remove the bread from the machine and let it cool on a wire rack before slicing.

Nutritional Value (Amount per Serving):

Calories: 169; Fat: 4.92; Carb: 25.45; Protein: 5.47

Grapefruit Rosemary Bread

Prep Time: 15 Minutes   Cook Time: 3 Hours   Serves: 10

Ingredients:

- 1/2 cup fresh grapefruit segments, chopped
- 2 tablespoons fresh rosemary leaves, finely chopped
- 1/4 cup unsalted butter, melted
- 1/2 cup granulated sugar
- 2 large eggs
- 1 teaspoon vanilla extract
- 2 cups all-purpose flour
- 1 1/2 teaspoons baking powder
- 1/2 teaspoon baking soda
- 1/4 teaspoon salt

Directions:

1. In a mixing bowl, combine chopped fresh grapefruit segments, finely chopped rosemary leaves, melted butter, sugar, eggs, and vanilla extract.
2. In a separate bowl, sift together all-purpose flour, baking powder, baking

soda, and salt.
3. Gradually add the dry ingredients to the wet ingredients, stirring until just combined.
4. Pour the batter into the bread machine pan.
5. Select the "Bake" program and the desired loaf size and crust shade.
6. Press Start to begin the baking cycle.
7. Once the cycle is complete, carefully remove the bread from the machine and let it cool on a wire rack before slicing.

Nutritional Value (Amount per Serving):

Calories: 155; Fat: 4.27; Carb: 25.59; Protein: 3.39

Orange Rolls

Prep Time: 15 Minutes   Cook Time: 3 Hours   Serves: 20

Ingredients:

- 1/4 cup heavy cream, warmed
- 1/2 cup orange juice concentrate
- 2 tbsp sugar1 tsp salt
- 1 large egg + 1 yolk
- 6 tbsp unsalted butter, softened
- 3 cups all-purpose flour
- 2 tsp bread machine yeast
- 2 tbsp unsalted butter, softened

- 1/2 cup sugar +2 Tbsp grated orange zest mixture
- 1/4 cup heavy cream
- 1/4 cup sugar
- 2 tbsp orange juice concentrate
- 2 ybsp unsalted butter
- 1/8 tsp salt

Directions:

1. Add each ingredient for the dough to the bread machine.
2. Select the Artisan Dough program and press Start.
3. When it is finished, the dough should have doubled in size.
4. Move the dough from the bread machine to a floured surface.
5. Roll the dough into rectangle. Cover it with butter and the sugar-orange zest mixture.
6. Roll the dough tightly from the long side. Cut into quarters. Then cut the quarters into 5 evenly-sized rolls.
7. Put them onto a greased pan, cover it with towel, and let them rise for 45 minutes in a warm place.
8. Bake at 325°F in a preheated oven for 25-30 minutes.
9. Add each of the icing ingredients to a saucepan. Mix and cook over a medium heat until the mixture is syrupy. Let it cool.
10. Pour icing over warm rolls and serve.

Nutritional Value (Amount per Serving):

Calories: 137; Fat: 6.19; Carb: 17.66; Protein: 2.65

Chapter 4: Almond Flour Gluten-free Breads

Almond Flour Gluten-Free Rosemary Garlic Bread

Prep Time: 20 Minutes   Cook Time: 2 Hours 55 Minutes   Serves: 8

Ingredients:

- 2 cups almond flour
- 1/4 cup coconut flour
- 1 tsp baking powder
- 1/2 tsp baking soda
- 1/2 tsp salt
- 1 tbsp finely chopped fresh rosemary
- 2 cloves garlic, minced
- 1/4 cup olive oil
- 4 large eggs
- 1 tbsp apple cider vinegar

Directions:

1. In a large bowl, combine almond flour, coconut flour, baking powder, baking soda, salt, chopped rosemary, and minced garlic.
2. In another bowl, whisk together olive oil, eggs, and apple cider vinegar until well combined.
3. Pour the wet ingredients into the dry ingredients and mix until a smooth batter forms.
4. Grease a loaf pan suitable for your Cuisinart Bread Machine and pour the batter into it, spreading it evenly.
5. Place the loaf pan into the bread machine and select the Gluten-Free program. Adjust crust shade and loaf size as preferred. Press Start to begin baking.
6. Once the bread is baked, remove the loaf pan from the machine and let it cool in the pan for about 10 minutes.
7. After 10 minutes, transfer the rosemary garlic bread from the loaf pan to a wire rack to cool completely before slicing.

Nutritional Value (Amount per Serving):

Calories: 93; Fat: 9.19; Carb: 1.25; Protein: 1.52

Almond Flour Gluten-Free Cinnamon Raisin Bread

Prep Time: 15 Minutes   Cook Time: 3 Hours 5 Minutes   Serves: 8

Ingredients:

- 2 cups almond flour
- 1/4 cup coconut flour
- 1 tsp baking powder
- 1/2 tsp baking soda
- 1/2 tsp salt
- 1 tsp ground cinnamon
- 1/2 cup raisins
- 1/4 cup honey or maple syrup
- 1/4 cup melted coconut oil
- 4 large eggs
- 1 tsp vanilla extract

Directions:

1. In a large bowl, mix together almond flour, coconut flour, baking powder,

baking soda, salt, ground cinnamon, and raisins.

2. In another bowl, combine honey (or maple syrup), melted coconut oil, eggs, and vanilla extract. Mix until well combined.

3. Pour the wet ingredients into the dry ingredients and stir until a smooth batter forms.

4. Grease a loaf pan suitable for your Cuisinart Bread Machine and pour the batter into it, spreading it evenly.

5. Place the loaf pan into the bread machine and select the Gluten-Free program. Adjust crust shade and loaf size as preferred. Press Start to begin baking.

6. Once the bread is baked, remove the loaf pan from the machine and let it cool in the pan for about 10 minutes.

7. After 10 minutes, transfer the cinnamon raisin bread from the loaf pan to a wire rack to cool completely before slicing.

Nutritional Value (Amount per Serving):

Calories: 118; Fat: 9.25; Carb: 7.9; Protein: 1.48

Almond Flour Gluten-Free Herb Focaccia

Prep Time: 25 Minutes   Cook Time: 2 Hours 45 Minutes   Serves: 8

Ingredients:

- 2 cups almond flour
- 1/4 cup coconut flour
- 1 tsp baking powder
- 1/2 tsp baking soda
- 1/2 tsp salt
- 1 tbsp finely chopped fresh rosemary
- 1 tbsp finely chopped fresh thyme
- 2 cloves garlic, minced
- 1/4 cup olive oil
- 4 large eggs
- 1 tbsp apple cider vinegar

Directions:

1. In a large bowl, combine almond flour, coconut flour, baking powder, baking soda, salt, chopped rosemary, chopped thyme, and minced garlic.

2. In another bowl, whisk together olive oil, eggs, and apple cider vinegar until well combined.

3. Pour the wet ingredients into the dry ingredients and mix until a smooth batter forms.

4. Grease a loaf pan suitable for your Cuisinart Bread Machine and pour the batter into it, spreading it evenly.

5. Place the loaf pan into the bread machine and select the Gluten-Free program. Adjust crust shade and loaf size as preferred. Press Start to begin baking.

6. Once the bread is baked, remove the loaf pan from the machine and let it

cool in the pan for about 10 minutes.

7. After 10 minutes, transfer the herb focaccia from the loaf pan to a wire rack to cool completely before slicing.

Nutritional Value (Amount per Serving):

Calories: 93; Fat: 9.19; Carb: 1.32; Protein: 1.54

Almond Flour Gluten-Free Sun-Dried Tomato Bread

Prep Time: 20 Minutes   Cook Time: 3 Hours 10 Minutes   Serves: 8

Ingredients:

- 2 cups almond flour
- 1/4 cup coconut flour
- 1 tsp baking powder
- 1/2 tsp baking soda
- 1/2 tsp salt
- 1/4 cup chopped sun-dried tomatoes
- (drained if oil-packed)
- 1/4 cup chopped fresh basil
- 2 cloves garlic, minced
- 1/4 cup olive oil
- 4 large eggs
- 1 tbsp apple cider vinegar

Directions:

1. In a large bowl, combine almond flour, coconut flour, baking powder, baking soda, salt, chopped sun-dried tomatoes, chopped basil, and minced garlic.
2. In another bowl, whisk together olive oil, eggs, and apple cider vinegar until well combined.
3. Pour the wet ingredients into the dry ingredients and mix until a smooth batter forms.
4. Grease a loaf pan suitable for your Cuisinart Bread Machine and pour the batter into it, spreading it evenly.
5. Place the loaf pan into the bread machine and select the Gluten-Free program. Adjust crust shade and loaf size as preferred. Press Start to begin baking.
6. Once the bread is baked, remove the loaf pan from the machine and let it cool in the pan for about 10 minutes.
7. After 10 minutes, transfer the sun-dried tomato bread from the loaf pan to a wire rack to cool completely before slicing.

Nutritional Value (Amount per Serving):

Calories: 97; Fat: 9.23; Carb: 2.17; Protein: 1.78

Almond Flour Gluten-Free Herb and Cheese Bread

Prep Time: 25 Minutes   Cook Time: 3 Hours 5 Minutes   Serves: 8

Ingredients:

- 2 cups almond flour
- 1/4 cup coconut flour
- 1 tsp baking powder
- 1/2 tsp baking soda
- 1/2 tsp salt
- 1 tbsp finely chopped fresh rosemary
- 1 tbsp finely chopped fresh thyme
- 1/2 cup grated Parmesan cheese
- 1/4 cup grated mozzarella cheese
- 1/4 cup olive oil
- 4 large eggs
- 1 tbsp apple cider vinegar

Directions:

1. In a large bowl, combine almond flour, coconut flour, baking powder, baking soda, salt, chopped rosemary, chopped thyme, grated Parmesan cheese, and grated mozzarella cheese.
2. In another bowl, whisk together olive oil, eggs, and apple cider vinegar until well combined.
3. Pour the wet ingredients into the dry ingredients and mix until a smooth batter forms.
4. Grease a loaf pan suitable for your Cuisinart Bread Machine and pour the batter into it, spreading it evenly.
5. Place the loaf pan into the bread machine and select the Gluten-Free program. Adjust crust shade and loaf size as preferred. Press Start to begin baking.
6. Once the bread is baked, remove the loaf pan from the machine and let it cool in the pan for about 10 minutes.
7. After 10 minutes, transfer the herb and cheese bread from the loaf pan to a wire rack to cool completely before slicing.

Nutritional Value (Amount per Serving):

Calories: 123; Fat: 10.93; Carb: 2.07; Protein: 4.39

Almond Flour Gluten-Free Cranberry Orange Bread

Prep Time: 15 Minutes   Cook Time: 3 Hours   Serves: 8

Ingredients:

- 2 cups almond flour
- 1/4 cup coconut flour
- 1 tsp baking powder
- 1/2 tsp baking soda
- 1/2 tsp salt
- Zest of 1 orange
- 1/2 cup dried cranberries
- 1/4 cup honey or maple syrup
- 1/4 cup melted coconut oil
- 4 large eggs
- 1/4 cup fresh orange juice
- 1 tsp vanilla extract

Directions:

1. In a large bowl, combine almond flour, coconut flour, baking powder,

baking soda, salt, orange zest, and dried cranberries.

2. In another bowl, whisk together honey (or maple syrup), melted coconut oil, eggs, orange juice, and vanilla extract until well combined.

3. Pour the wet ingredients into the dry ingredients and mix until a smooth batter forms.

4. Grease a loaf pan suitable for your Cuisinart Bread Machine and pour the batter into it, spreading it evenly.

5. Place the loaf pan into the bread machine and select the Gluten-Free program. Adjust crust shade and loaf size as preferred. Press Start to begin baking.

6. Once the bread is baked, remove the loaf pan from the machine and let it cool in the pan for about 10 minutes.

7. After 10 minutes, transfer the cranberry orange bread from the loaf pan to a wire rack to cool completely before slicing.

Nutritional Value (Amount per Serving):

Calories: 145; Fat: 9.3; Carb: 14.24; Protein: 1.74

Almond Flour Gluten-Free Chocolate Chip Banana Bread

Prep Time: 20 Minutes   Cook Time: 2 Hours 50 Minutes   Serves: 8

Ingredients:

- 2 cups almond flour
- 1/4 cup coconut flour
- 1 tsp baking powder
- 1/2 tsp baking soda
- 1/2 tsp salt
- 3 ripe bananas, mashed
- 1/4 cup honey or maple syrup
- 1/4 cup melted coconut oil
- 4 large eggs
- 1 tsp vanilla extract
- 1/2 cup gluten-free chocolate chips

Directions:

1. In a large bowl, combine almond flour, coconut flour, baking powder, baking soda, salt, mashed bananas, honey (or maple syrup), melted coconut oil, eggs, and vanilla extract.

2. Stir in gluten-free chocolate chips until evenly distributed.

3. Grease a loaf pan suitable for your Cuisinart Bread Machine and pour the batter into it, spreading it evenly.

4. Place the loaf pan into the bread machine and select the Gluten-Free program. Adjust crust shade and loaf size as preferred. Press Start to begin baking.

5. Once the bread is baked, remove the loaf pan from the machine and let it cool in the pan for about 10 minutes.

6. After 10 minutes, transfer the chocolate chip banana bread from the loaf pan to a wire rack to cool completely before slicing.

Nutritional Value (Amount per Serving):

Calories: 181; Fat: 11.51; Carb: 19.03; Protein: 2.23

Almond Flour Gluten-Free Herb and Olive Focaccia

Prep Time: 25 Minutes   Cook Time: 2 Hours 45 Minutes   Serves: 8

Ingredients:

- 2 cups almond flour
- 1/4 cup coconut flour
- 1 tsp baking powder
- 1/2 tsp baking soda
- 1/2 tsp salt
- 1 tbsp finely chopped fresh rosemary
- 1 tbsp finely chopped fresh thyme
- 1/2 cup sliced olives (black or green)
- 1/4 cup olive oil
- 4 large eggs
- 1 tbsp apple cider vinegar

Directions:

1. In a large bowl, combine almond flour, coconut flour, baking powder, baking soda, salt, chopped rosemary, chopped thyme, and sliced olives.
2. In another bowl, whisk together olive oil, eggs, and apple cider vinegar until well combined.
3. Pour the wet ingredients into the dry ingredients and mix until a smooth batter forms.
4. Grease a loaf pan suitable for your Cuisinart Bread Machine and pour the batter into it, spreading it evenly.
5. Place the loaf pan into the bread machine and select the Gluten-Free program. Adjust crust shade and loaf size as preferred. Press Start to begin baking.
6. Once the bread is baked, remove the loaf pan from the machine and let it cool in the pan for about 10 minutes.
7. After 10 minutes, transfer the herb and olive focaccia from the loaf pan to a wire rack to cool completely before slicing.

Nutritional Value (Amount per Serving):

Calories: 101; Fat: 10.09; Carb: 1.6; Protein: 1.56

Almond Flour Gluten-Free Herb and Garlic Breadsticks

Prep Time: 20 Minutes   Cook Time: 2 Hours 45 Minutes   Serves: 8

Ingredients:

- 2 cups almond flour
- 1/4 cup coconut flour
- 1 tsp baking powder
- 1/2 tsp baking soda
- 1/2 tsp salt
- 1 tbsp finely chopped fresh rosemary
- 1 tbsp finely chopped fresh thyme
- 2 cloves garlic, minced
- 1/4 cup olive oil
- 4 large eggs
- 1 tbsp apple cider vinegar

Directions:

1. In a large bowl, combine almond flour, coconut flour, baking powder, baking soda, salt, chopped rosemary, chopped thyme, and minced garlic.
2. In another bowl, whisk together olive oil, eggs, and apple cider vinegar until well combined.
3. Pour the wet ingredients into the dry ingredients and mix until a smooth batter forms.
4. Grease a baking sheet suitable for the bread machine, or line it with parchment paper.
5. Scoop the batter onto the baking sheet, forming breadsticks about 4 inches long and 1 inch wide. Leave space between each breadstick.
6. Place the baking sheet into the bread machine and select the Gluten-Free program. Adjust crust shade as preferred. Press Start to begin baking.
7. Once the breadsticks are baked, remove them from the machine and let them cool on the baking sheet for about 10 minutes.
8. After 10 minutes, transfer the breadsticks to a wire rack to cool completely before serving.

Nutritional Value (Amount per Serving):

Calories: 93; Fat: 9.19; Carb: 1.32; Protein: 1.54

Almond Flour Gluten-Free Apple Cinnamon Bread

Prep Time: 20 Minutes   Cook Time: 3 Hours   Serves: 8

Ingredients:

- 2 cups almond flour
- 1/4 cup coconut flour
- 1 tsp baking powder
- 1/2 tsp baking soda
- 1/2 tsp salt
- 1 tsp ground cinnamon
- 2 medium apples, peeled and diced
- 1/4 cup honey or maple syrup
- 1/4 cup melted coconut oil
- 4 large eggs
- 1 tsp vanilla extract

Directions:

1. In a large bowl, combine almond flour, coconut flour, baking powder,

baking soda, salt, and ground cinnamon.

2. In another bowl, mix together diced apples, honey (or maple syrup), melted coconut oil, eggs, and vanilla extract until well combined.

3. Pour the wet ingredients into the dry ingredients and mix until a smooth batter forms.

4. Grease a loaf pan suitable for your Cuisinart Bread Machine and pour the batter into it, spreading it evenly.

5. Place the loaf pan into the bread machine and select the Gluten-Free program. Adjust crust shade and loaf size as preferred. Press Start to begin baking.

6. Once the bread is baked, remove the loaf pan from the machine and let it cool in the pan for about 10 minutes.

7. After 10 minutes, transfer the apple cinnamon bread from the loaf pan to a wire rack to cool completely before slicing..

Nutritional Value (Amount per Serving):

Calories: 141; Fat: 9.32; Carb: 14.16; Protein: 1.6

Almond Flour Gluten-Free Carrot Cake Bread

Prep Time: 25 Minutes   Cook Time: 3 Hours 5 Minutes   Serves: 8

Ingredients:

- 2 cups almond flour
- 1/4 cup coconut flour
- 1 tsp baking powder
- 1/2 tsp baking soda
- 1/2 tsp salt
- 1 tsp ground cinnamon
- 1/2 tsp ground nutmeg

- 1/4 tsp ground cloves
- 1 cup grated carrots
- 1/4 cup honey or maple syrup
- 1/4 cup melted coconut oil
- 4 large eggs
- 1 tsp vanilla extract

Directions:

1. In a large bowl, combine almond flour, coconut flour, baking powder, baking soda, salt, ground cinnamon, ground nutmeg, and ground cloves.

2. In another bowl, mix together grated carrots, honey (or maple syrup), melted coconut oil, eggs, and vanilla extract until well combined.

3. Pour the wet ingredients into the dry ingredients and mix until a smooth batter forms.

4. Grease a loaf pan suitable for your Cuisinart Bread Machine and pour the batter into it, spreading it evenly.

5. Place the loaf pan into the bread machine and select the Gluten-Free program. Adjust crust shade and loaf size as preferred. Press Start to begin baking.

6. Once the bread is baked, remove the loaf pan from the machine and let it cool in the pan for about 10 minutes.
7. After 10 minutes, transfer the carrot cake bread from the loaf pan to a wire rack to cool completely before slicing.

Nutritional Value (Amount per Serving):

Calories: 125; Fat: 9.4; Carb: 9.26; Protein: 1.79

Almond Flour Gluten-Free Banana Bread

Prep Time: 15 Minutes   Cook Time: 3 Hours   Serves: 6

Ingredients:

- 2 ripe bananas, mashed
- 1/4 cup honey or maple syrup
- 1/4 cup unsweetened applesauce
- 1/4 cup coconut oil, melted
- 2 large eggs
- 1 tsp vanilla extract
- 2 cups almond flour
- 1/4 cup tapioca flour or arrowroot powder
- 1 tsp baking powder
- 1/2 tsp baking soda
- 1/2 tsp cinnamon
- 1/4 tsp salt
- Optional: 1/2 cup chopped nuts or chocolate chips

Directions:

1. In a large mixing bowl, combine mashed bananas, honey or maple syrup, applesauce, melted coconut oil, eggs, and vanilla extract.
2. In a separate bowl, whisk together almond flour, tapioca flour or arrowroot powder, baking powder, baking soda, cinnamon, and salt.
3. Gradually add the dry ingredients to the wet ingredients, mixing until well combined. Fold in chopped nuts or chocolate chips if desired.
4. Pour the batter into a greased loaf pan.
5. Place the loaf pan into the Cuisinart Bread Machine.
6. Select the Gluten-Free program, setting crust shade and loaf size as desired, then press Start.
7. Once the bread is done, remove it from the bread machine and let it cool in the pan for 10 minutes. Then transfer it to a wire rack to cool completely before slicing.

Nutritional Value (Amount per Serving):

Calories: 216; Fat: 13.31; Carb: 24.48; Protein: 1.5

Chapter 5: Spice and Nut Breads

Chai Spiced Bread

Prep Time: 20 Minutes   Cook Time: 3 Hours   Serves: 8

Ingredients:

- 2 cups all-purpose flour
- 1 tbsp chai spice blend (store-bought or homemade)
- 1/4 tsp salt
- 2 tbsp granulated sugar
- 1 packet (2 1/4 tsp) active dry yeast
- 1/2 cup warm water
- 1/4 cup honey
- 2 tbsp unsalted butter, melted
- 1/4 cup chopped almonds

Directions:

1. In a large mixing bowl, combine flour, chai spice blend, salt, and granulated sugar. Mix well.
2. In a separate small bowl, dissolve yeast in warm water. Let it sit for 5 minutes until foamy.
3. Add honey and melted butter to the yeast mixture and stir to combine.
4. Pour the wet ingredients into the dry ingredients and mix until a dough forms.
5. Fold in the chopped almonds until evenly distributed throughout the dough.
6. Grease a loaf pan and transfer the dough into it, shaping it evenly.
7. Place the loaf pan into the Cuisinart Bread Machine.
8. Select the White program and set crust shade and loaf size as desired. Press Start.
9. Once the bread is done, remove it from the bread machine and let it cool in the pan for 10 minutes. Then transfer it to a wire rack to cool completely before slicing.

Nutritional Value (Amount per Serving):

Calories: 177; Fat: 2.41; Carb: 35.44; Protein: 3.79

Maple Walnut Bread

Prep Time: 15 Minutes   Cook Time: 3 Hours   Serves: 8

Ingredients:

- 1/2 cup pure maple syrup
- 1/2 cup chopped walnuts
- 2 cups bread flour
- 1 tsp ground cinnamon

- 1/4 tsp salt
- 2 tbsp brown sugar
- 1 packet (2 1/4 tsp) active dry yeast
- 1/2 cup warm milk
- 2 tbsp unsalted butter, melted

Directions:

1. In a small saucepan, warm the maple syrup over low heat until slightly heated. Remove from heat and let it cool.
2. In a large mixing bowl, combine bread flour, cinnamon, salt, and brown sugar. Mix well.
3. In a separate small bowl, dissolve yeast in warm milk. Let it sit for 5 minutes until foamy.
4. Add melted butter and cooled maple syrup to the yeast mixture and stir to combine.
5. Pour the wet ingredients into the dry ingredients and mix until a dough forms.
6. Fold in the chopped walnuts until evenly distributed throughout the dough.
7. Grease a loaf pan and transfer the dough into it, shaping it evenly.
8. Place the loaf pan into the Cuisinart Bread Machine.
9. Select the White program and set crust shade and loaf size as desired. Press Start.
10. Once the bread is done, remove it from the bread machine and let it cool in the pan for 10 minutes. Then transfer it to a wire rack to cool completely before slicing.

Nutritional Value (Amount per Serving):

Calories: 239; Fat: 6.14; Carb: 40.88; Protein: 5.87

Orange Cranberry Walnut Bread

Prep Time: 15 Minutes   Cook Time: 3 Hours   Serves: 8

Ingredients:

- 1 cup dried cranberries
- 1/2 cup chopped walnuts
- 2 cups all-purpose flour
- 1 tbsp orange zest
- 1/4 tsp salt
- 2 tbsp granulated sugar
- 1 packet (2 1/4 tsp) active dry yeast
- 1/2 cup warm water
- 1/4 cup freshly squeezed orange juice
- 2 tbsp vegetable oil

Directions:

1. In a small bowl, soak dried cranberries in warm water for 10 minutes. Drain well and set aside.
2. In a large mixing bowl, combine flour, orange zest, salt, and granulated sugar. Mix well.
3. In a separate small bowl, dissolve yeast in warm water. Let it sit for 5 minutes until foamy.
4. Add orange juice and vegetable oil to the yeast mixture and stir to combine.
5. Pour the wet ingredients into the dry ingredients and mix until a dough forms.
6. Fold in the soaked dried cranberries and chopped walnuts until evenly distributed throughout the dough.
7. Grease a loaf pan and transfer the dough into it, shaping it evenly.
8. Place the loaf pan into the Cuisinart Bread Machine.
9. Select the Sweet program and set crust shade and loaf size as desired. Press Start.
10. Once the bread is done, remove it from the bread machine and let it cool in the pan for 10 minutes. Then transfer it to a wire rack to cool completely before slicing.

Nutritional Value (Amount per Serving):

Calories: 209; Fat: 7.08; Carb: 32.3; Protein: 4.42

Pumpkin Spice Pecan Bread

Prep Time: 15 Minutes   Cook Time: 3 Hours   Serves: 8

Ingredients:

- 1 cup canned pumpkin puree
- 1/2 cup chopped pecans
- 2 cups bread flour
- 1 tsp ground cinnamon
- 1/2 tsp ground nutmeg
- 1/4 tsp ground cloves
- 1/4 tsp ground ginger
- 1/4 tsp salt
- 2 tbsp brown sugar
- 1 packet (2 1/4 tsp) active dry yeast
- 1/2 cup warm milk
- 2 tbsp unsalted butter, melted

Directions:

1. In a large mixing bowl, combine bread flour, cinnamon, nutmeg, cloves, ginger, salt, and brown sugar. Mix well.
2. In a separate small bowl, dissolve yeast in warm milk. Let it sit for 5 minutes until foamy.
3. Add melted butter and pumpkin puree to the yeast mixture and stir to combine.

4. Pour the wet ingredients into the dry ingredients and mix until a dough forms.
5. Fold in the chopped pecans until evenly distributed throughout the dough.
6. Grease a loaf pan and transfer the dough into it, shaping it evenly.
7. Place the loaf pan into the Cuisinart Bread Machine.
8. Select the Whole Wheat program and set crust shade and loaf size as desired. Press Start.
9. Once the bread is done, remove it from the bread machine and let it cool in the pan for 10 minutes. Then transfer it to a wire rack to cool completely before slicing.

Nutritional Value (Amount per Serving):

Calories: 211; Fat: 7.53; Carb: 30.44; Protein: 6.19

Apple Cinnamon Walnut Bread

Prep Time: 15 Minutes   Cook Time: 3 Hours   Serves: 8

Ingredients:

- 1 cup diced apples (peeled and cored)
- 1/2 cup chopped walnuts
- 2 cups all-purpose flour
- 1 tsp ground cinnamon
- 1/2 tsp ground nutmeg
- 1/4 tsp ground cloves
- 1/4 tsp salt
- 2 tbsp granulated sugar
- 1 packet (2 1/4 tsp) active dry yeast
- 1/2 cup warm water
- 1/4 cup unsweetened applesauce
- 2 tbsp vegetable oil

Directions:

1. In a small bowl, toss diced apples with a sprinkle of cinnamon. Set aside.
2. In a large mixing bowl, combine flour, cinnamon, nutmeg, cloves, salt, and granulated sugar. Mix well.
3. In a separate small bowl, dissolve yeast in warm water. Let it sit for 5 minutes until foamy.
4. Add applesauce and vegetable oil to the yeast mixture and stir to combine.
5. Pour the wet ingredients into the dry ingredients and mix until a dough forms.
6. Fold in the diced apples and chopped walnuts until evenly distributed throughout the dough.

7. Grease a loaf pan and transfer the dough into it, shaping it evenly.
8. Place the loaf pan into the Cuisinart Bread Machine.
9. Select the Sweet program and set crust shade and loaf size as desired. Press Start.
10. Once the bread is done, remove it from the bread machine and let it cool in the pan for 10 minutes. Then transfer it to a wire rack to cool completely before slicing.

Nutritional Value (Amount per Serving):

Calories: 200; Fat: 7.19; Carb: 29.97; Protein: 4.6

Hazelnut Chocolate Swirl Bread

Prep Time: 20 Minutes   Cook Time: 3 Hours   Serves: 8

Ingredients:

- 1/2 cup chopped hazelnuts
- 2 cups bread flour
- 1/4 cup cocoa powder
- 1/4 cup granulated sugar
- 1 tsp instant coffee granules
- 1/2 tsp salt
- 1 packet (2 1/4 tsp) active dry yeast
- 1/2 cup warm milk
- 1/4 cup unsalted butter, melted
- 1 large egg
- 1/4 cup chocolate chips

Directions:

1. In a small bowl, toss chopped hazelnuts with a sprinkle of cocoa powder. Set aside.
2. In a large mixing bowl, combine bread flour, cocoa powder, sugar, instant coffee, and salt. Mix well.
3. In a separate small bowl, dissolve yeast in warm milk. Let it sit for 5 minutes until foamy.
4. Add melted butter and egg to the yeast mixture and stir to combine.
5. Pour the wet ingredients into the dry ingredients and mix until a dough forms.
6. Fold in the chopped hazelnuts and chocolate chips until evenly distributed throughout the dough.
7. Grease a loaf pan and transfer half of the dough into it, spreading it evenly.
8. Sprinkle half of the hazelnut-chocolate mixture over the dough.
9. Repeat with the remaining dough and hazelnut-chocolate mixture.
10. Use a knife to swirl the layers together gently.
11. Place the loaf pan into the Cuisinart Bread Machine.
12. Select the White program and set crust shade and loaf size as desired. Press Start.
13. Once the bread is done, remove it from the bread machine and let it

cool in the pan for 10 minutes. Then transfer it to a wire rack to cool completely before slicing.

Nutritional Value (Amount per Serving):

Calories: 273; Fat: 10.94; Carb: 38.22; Protein: 7.48

Gingerbread Loaf

Prep Time: 20 Minutes   Cook Time: 3 Hours   Serves: 8

Ingredients:

- 2 cups all-purpose flour
- 1 tsp ground ginger
- 1 tsp ground cinnamon
- 1/2 tsp ground cloves
- 1/4 tsp ground nutmeg
- 1/4 tsp salt
- 2 tsp baking powder
- 1/2 cup brown sugar
- 1 packet (2 1/4 tsp) active dry yeast
- 1/2 cup warm milk
- 1/4 cup molasses
- 1/4 cup unsalted butter, melted
- 1 large egg

Directions:

1. In a large mixing bowl, combine flour, ginger, cinnamon, cloves, nutmeg, salt, baking powder, and brown sugar. Mix well.
2. In a separate small bowl, dissolve yeast in warm milk. Let it sit for 5 minutes until foamy.
3. Add molasses, melted butter, and egg to the yeast mixture and stir to combine.
4. Pour the wet ingredients into the dry ingredients and mix until a dough forms.
5. Grease a loaf pan and transfer the dough into it, shaping it evenly.
6. Place the loaf pan into the Cuisinart Bread Machine.
7. Select the Whole Wheat program and set crust shade and loaf size as desired. Press Start.
8. Once the bread is done, remove it from the bread machine and let it cool in the pan for 10 minutes. Then transfer it to a wire rack to cool completely before slicing.

Nutritional Value (Amount per Serving):

Calories: 255; Fat: 5.29; Carb: 47.43; Protein: 5.07

Walnut Honey Oat Bread

Prep Time: 15 Minutes   Cook Time: 3 Hours   Serves: 8

Ingredients:

- 1/2 cup chopped walnuts
- 1/4 cup honey
- 1/2 cup old-fashioned oats
- 2 cups bread flour
- 1/2 cup whole wheat flour
- 1 tsp salt
- 1 packet (2 1/4 tsp) active dry yeast
- 1/2 cup warm water
- 1/4 cup milk
- 2 tbsp unsalted butter, melted

Directions:

1. In a small bowl, toss chopped walnuts with honey until evenly coated. Set aside.
2. In a large mixing bowl, combine oats, bread flour, whole wheat flour, and salt. Mix well.
3. In a separate small bowl, dissolve yeast in warm water. Let it sit for 5 minutes until foamy.
4. Add milk and melted butter to the yeast mixture and stir to combine.
5. Pour the wet ingredients into the dry ingredients and mix until a dough forms.
6. Fold in the honey-coated walnuts until evenly distributed throughout the dough.
7. Grease a loaf pan and transfer the dough into it, shaping it evenly.
8. Place the loaf pan into the Cuisinart Bread Machine.
9. Select the Whole Wheat program and set crust shade and loaf size as desired. Press Start.
10. Once the bread is done, remove it from the bread machine and let it cool in the pan for 10 minutes. Then transfer it to a wire rack to cool completely before slicing.

Nutritional Value (Amount per Serving):

Calories: 254; Fat: 6.68; Carb: 44.29; Protein: 7.62

Apricot Ginger Pecan Bread

Prep Time: 15 Minutes   Cook Time: 3 Hours   Serves: 8

Ingredients:

- 1 cup chopped dried apricots
- 1/2 cup chopped pecans
- 2 cups bread flour
- 1 tsp ground ginger
- 1/2 tsp ground cinnamon
- 1/4 tsp ground cloves
- 1/4 tsp salt
- 2 tbsp granulated sugar
- 1 packet (2 1/4 tsp) active dry yeast
- 1/2 cup warm water
- 1/4 cup unsweetened applesauce
- 2 tbsp vegetable oil

Directions:

1. In a small bowl, soak chopped dried apricots in warm water for 10 minutes. Drain well and set aside.
2. In a large mixing bowl, combine bread flour, ginger, cinnamon, cloves, salt, and granulated sugar. Mix well.
3. In a separate small bowl, dissolve yeast in warm water. Let it sit for 5 minutes until foamy.
4. Add applesauce and vegetable oil to the yeast mixture and stir to combine.
5. Pour the wet ingredients into the dry ingredients and mix until a dough forms.
6. Fold in the soaked dried apricots and chopped pecans until evenly distributed throughout the dough.
7. Grease a loaf pan and transfer the dough into it, shaping it evenly.
8. Place the loaf pan into the Cuisinart Bread Machine.
9. Select the Sweet program and set crust shade and loaf size as desired. Press Start.
10. Once the bread is done, remove it from the bread machine and let it cool in the pan for 10 minutes. Then transfer it to a wire rack to cool completely before slicing.

Nutritional Value (Amount per Serving):

Calories: 252; Fat: 8.66; Carb: 39.4; Protein: 5.8

Cranberry Orange Pecan Bread

Prep Time: 15 Minutes   Cook Time: 3 Hours   Serves: 8

Ingredients:

- 1 cup dried cranberries
- 1/2 cup chopped pecans
- 2 cups all-purpose flour
- 1 tbsp orange zest
- 1/4 tsp salt
- 2 tbsp granulated sugar
- 1 packet (2 1/4 tsp) active dry yeast
- 1/2 cup warm water
- 1/4 cup freshly squeezed orange juice
- 2 tbsp vegetable oil

Directions:

1. In a small bowl, soak dried cranberries in warm water for 10 minutes. Drain well and set aside.
2. In a large mixing bowl, combine flour, orange zest, salt, and granulated sugar. Mix well.
3. In a separate small bowl, dissolve yeast in warm water. Let it sit for 5 minutes until foamy.
4. Add orange juice and vegetable oil to the yeast mixture and stir to combine.
5. Pour the wet ingredients into the dry ingredients and mix until a dough forms.

6. Fold in the soaked dried cranberries and chopped pecans until evenly distributed throughout the dough.
7. Grease a loaf pan and transfer the dough into it, shaping it evenly.
8. Place the loaf pan into the Cuisinart Bread Machine.
9. Select the Sweet program and set crust shade and loaf size as desired. Press Start.
10. Once the bread is done, remove it from the bread machine and let it cool in the pan for 10 minutes. Then transfer it to a wire rack to cool completely before slicing.

Nutritional Value (Amount per Serving):

Calories: 219; Fat: 8.27; Carb: 32.47; Protein: 4.23

Carrot Walnut Bread

Prep Time: 20 Minutes   Cook Time: 3 Hours   Serves: 8

Ingredients:

- 1 cup grated carrots
- 1/2 cup chopped walnuts
- 2 cups all-purpose flour
- 1 tsp ground cinnamon
- 1/2 tsp ground nutmeg
- 1/4 tsp ground cloves
- 1/4 tsp salt
- 2 tbsp granulated sugar
- 1 packet (2 1/4 tsp) active dry yeast
- 1/2 cup warm water
- 1/4 cup unsweetened applesauce
- 2 tbsp vegetable oil

Directions:

1. In a large mixing bowl, combine flour, cinnamon, nutmeg, cloves, salt, and granulated sugar. Mix well.
2. In a separate small bowl, dissolve yeast in warm water. Let it sit for 5 minutes until foamy.
3. Add applesauce and vegetable oil to the yeast mixture and stir to combine.
4. Pour the wet ingredients into the dry ingredients and mix until a dough forms.
5. Fold in the grated carrots and chopped walnuts until evenly distributed throughout the dough.
6. Grease a loaf pan and transfer the dough into it, shaping it evenly.
7. Place the loaf pan into the Cuisinart Bread Machine.
8. Select the Sweet program and set crust shade and loaf size as desired. Press Start.
9. Once the bread is done, remove it from the bread machine and let it cool in the pan for 10 minutes. Then transfer it to a wire rack to cool completely before slicing.

Nutritional Value (Amount per Serving):

Calories: 199; Fat: 7.2; Carb: 29.41; Protein: 4.69

Chapter 6: Vegetable Breads

Pumpkin and Walnut Bread

Prep Time: 30 Minutes   Cook Time: 3 Hours   Serves: 8

Ingredients:

- 1 cup canned pumpkin puree
- 1/2 cup chopped walnuts
- 3 cups bread flour
- 2 teaspoons active dry yeast
- 1 teaspoon cinnamon
- 1/2 teaspoon nutmeg
- 1/2 teaspoon salt
- 1/4 cup brown sugar
- 1/4 cup olive oil
- 1/4 cup warm water (110°F)

Directions:

1. In a small bowl, dissolve brown sugar in warm water. Sprinkle yeast over the water and let it sit for about 5 minutes, until foamy.
2. In the bread machine pan, combine bread flour, cinnamon, nutmeg, salt, olive oil, and the yeast mixture.
3. Add canned pumpkin puree and chopped walnuts on top of the flour mixture.
4. Place the bread machine pan into the machine. Select the "Whole Wheat" program and set crust shade and loaf size as desired. Press Start.
5. Once the bread is done, remove it from the bread machine and let it cool in the pan for 10 minutes. Then transfer it to a wire rack to cool completely before slicing.

Nutritional Value (Amount per Serving):

Calories: 319; Fat: 11.08; Carb: 47.91; Protein: 7.69

Sweet Potato and Rosemary Bread

Prep Time: 25 Minutes   Cook Time: 3 Hours   Serves: 8

Ingredients:

- 1 cup mashed sweet potatoes
- 2 tablespoons chopped fresh rosemary
- 3 cups bread flour
- 2 teaspoons active dry yeast
- 1 teaspoon salt
- 1 tablespoon honey
- 1/4 cup olive oil
- 1/4 cup warm water (110°F)

Directions:

1. In a small bowl, dissolve honey in warm water. Sprinkle yeast over the water and let it sit for about 5 minutes, until foamy.
2. In the bread machine pan, combine bread flour, chopped rosemary, salt, olive oil, and the yeast mixture.
3. Add mashed sweet potatoes on top of the flour mixture.

4. Place the bread machine pan into the machine. Select the "Whole Wheat" program and set crust shade and loaf size as desired. Press Start.
5. Once the bread is done, remove it from the bread machine and let it cool in the pan for 10 minutes. Then transfer it to a wire rack to cool completely before slicing.

Nutritional Value (Amount per Serving):

Calories: 259; Fat: 7.73; Carb: 40.13; Protein: 6.69

Broccoli and Cheddar Bread

Prep Time: 20 Minutes   Cook Time: 3 Hours   Serves: 8

Ingredients:

- 1 cup finely chopped broccoli florets
- 1/2 cup shredded cheddar cheese
- 3 cups bread flour
- 2 teaspoons active dry yeast
- 1 teaspoon garlic powder
- 1 teaspoon salt
- 1 tablespoon olive oil
- 1 cup warm water (110°F)

Directions:

1. In a small bowl, dissolve garlic powder in warm water. Sprinkle yeast over the water and let it sit for about 5 minutes, until foamy.
2. In the bread machine pan, combine bread flour, salt, olive oil, and the yeast mixture.
3. Add finely chopped broccoli florets and shredded cheddar cheese on top of the flour mixture.
4. Place the bread machine pan into the machine. Select the "Artisan Dough" program and set crust shade and loaf size as desired. Press Start.
5. Once the dough is done, remove it from the bread machine and transfer it to a lightly floured surface.
6. Punch down the dough and shape it into a loaf. Place the loaf into a greased loaf pan.
7. Cover the loaf pan with a clean kitchen towel and let it rise in a warm place for about 30-45 minutes, until doubled in size.
8. Preheat the oven to 375°F. Bake the bread for 25-30 minutes, until golden brown and hollow-sounding when tapped on the bottom.
9. Remove the bread from the oven and let it cool in the pan for 10 minutes. Then transfer it to a wire rack to cool completely before slicing.

Nutritional Value (Amount per Serving):

Calories: 231; Fat: 3.9; Carb: 39.62; Protein: 8.68

Cornbread with Jalapeno and Cheddar

Prep Time: 15 Minutes   Cook Time: 3 Hours   Serves: 8

Ingredients:

- 1 cup cornmeal
- 1 cup all-purpose flour
- 1/2 cup shredded cheddar cheese
- 1 jalapeno pepper, seeded and finely chopped
- 2 teaspoons baking powder
- 1/2 teaspoon salt
- 1 cup buttermilk
- 1/4 cup olive oil
- 2 large eggs

Directions:

1. In a large bowl, whisk together cornmeal, all-purpose flour, baking powder, and salt.
2. In a separate bowl, beat eggs. Add buttermilk and olive oil, and whisk until well combined.
3. Pour the wet ingredients into the dry ingredients and mix until just combined.
4. Fold in shredded cheddar cheese and chopped jalapeno pepper.
5. Grease a loaf pan and pour the batter into it, smoothing the top with a spatula.
6. Place the loaf pan into the Cuisinart Bread Machine.
7. Select the "Cake" program and set crust shade and loaf size as desired. Press Start.
8. Once the bread is done, remove it from the bread machine and let it cool in the pan for 10 minutes. Then transfer it to a wire rack to cool completely before slicing.

Nutritional Value (Amount per Serving):

Calories: 242; Fat: 9.91; Carb: 31.35; Protein: 6.62

Onion and Herb Focaccia

Prep Time: 20 Minutes   Cook Time: 3 Hours   Serves: 8

Ingredients:

- 1 large onion, thinly sliced
- 2 tablespoons chopped fresh herbs (such as rosemary, thyme, or oregano)
- 3 cups bread flour

- 2 teaspoons active dry yeast
- 1 teaspoon salt
- 1/4 cup olive oil, plus more for drizzling
- 1 1/4 cups warm water (110°F)
- Coarse sea salt, for sprinkling

Directions:

1. In a small bowl, dissolve salt in warm water. Sprinkle yeast over the water and let it sit for about 5 minutes, until foamy.
2. In the bread machine pan, combine bread flour, olive oil, and the yeast mixture.
3. Add thinly sliced onion and chopped fresh herbs on top of the flour mixture.
4. Place the bread machine pan into the machine. Select the "Artisan Dough" program and set crust shade and loaf size as desired. Press Start.
5. Once the dough is done, remove it from the bread machine and transfer it to a lightly oiled baking sheet.
6. Press the dough out into a rectangle or round shape, about 1/2 inch thick.
7. Cover the dough with a clean kitchen towel and let it rise in a warm place for about 30-45 minutes, until slightly puffed.
8. Preheat the oven to 400°F. Drizzle olive oil over the top of the focaccia and sprinkle with coarse sea salt.
9. Bake the focaccia for 20-25 minutes, until golden brown and crispy on the edges.
10. Remove the focaccia from the oven and let it cool on the baking sheet for 5 minutes. Then transfer it to a wire rack to cool completely before slicing.

Nutritional Value (Amount per Serving):

Calories: 305; Fat: 12.47; Carb: 38.1; Protein: 9.5

Roasted Garlic and Rosemary Bread

Prep Time: 30 Minutes   Cook Time: 3 Hours   Serves: 8

Ingredients:

- 1/2 cup roasted garlic cloves, mashed
- 2 tablespoons chopped fresh rosemary
- 3 cups bread flour
- 2 teaspoons active dry yeast
- 1 teaspoon salt
- 1 tablespoon olive oil
- 1 cup warm water (110°F)

Directions:

1. In a small bowl, dissolve salt in warm water. Sprinkle yeast over the water and let it sit for about 5 minutes, until foamy.

2. In the bread machine pan, combine bread flour, chopped rosemary, olive oil, and the yeast mixture.
3. Add mashed roasted garlic cloves on top of the flour mixture.
4. Place the bread machine pan into the machine. Select the "Artisan Dough" program and set crust shade and loaf size as desired. Press Start.
5. Once the dough is done, remove it from the bread machine and transfer it to a lightly floured surface.
6. Punch down the dough and shape it into a loaf. Place the loaf into a greased loaf pan.
7. Cover the loaf pan with a clean kitchen towel and let it rise in a warm place for about 30-45 minutes, until doubled in size.
8. Preheat the oven to 375°F. Bake the bread for 25-30 minutes, until golden brown and hollow-sounding when tapped on the bottom.
9. Remove the bread from the oven and let it cool in the pan for 10 minutes. Then transfer it to a wire rack to cool completely before slicing.

Nutritional Value (Amount per Serving):

Calories: 217; Fat: 2.68; Carb: 40.57; Protein: 7.11

Kale and Parmesan Bread

Prep Time: 25 Minutes   Cook Time: 3 Hours   Serves: 8

Ingredients:

- 1 cup finely chopped kale leaves
- 1/2 cup grated Parmesan cheese
- 3 cups bread flour
- 2 teaspoons active dry yeast
- 1 teaspoon salt
- 1 tablespoon olive oil
- 1 cup warm water (110°F)

Directions:

1. In a small bowl, dissolve salt in warm water. Sprinkle yeast over the water and let it sit for about 5 minutes, until foamy.
2. In the bread machine pan, combine bread flour, olive oil, and the yeast mixture.
3. Add finely chopped kale leaves and grated Parmesan cheese on top of the flour mixture.
4. Place the bread machine pan into the machine. Select the "Artisan Dough" program and set crust shade and loaf size as desired. Press Start.
5. Once the dough is done, remove it from the bread machine and transfer it to a lightly floured surface.
6. Punch down the dough and shape it into a loaf. Place the loaf into a greased loaf pan.
7. Cover the loaf pan with a clean kitchen towel and let it rise in a warm place

for about 30-45 minutes, until doubled in size.

8. Preheat the oven to 375°F. Bake the bread for 25-30 minutes, until golden brown and hollow-sounding when tapped on the bottom.

9. Remove the bread from the oven and let it cool in the pan for 10 minutes. Then transfer it to a wire rack to cool completely before slicing.

Nutritional Value (Amount per Serving):

Calories: 231; Fat: 4.38; Carb: 38.72; Protein: 8.42

Butternut Squash and Sage Bread

Prep Time: 30 Minutes　　Cook Time: 3 Hours　　Serves: 8

Ingredients:

- 1 cup mashed butternut squash
- 2 tablespoons chopped fresh sage
- 3 cups bread flour
- 2 teaspoons active dry yeast
- 1 teaspoon salt
- 1 tablespoon honey
- 1/4 cup olive oil
- 1/4 cup warm water (110°F)

Directions:

1. In a small bowl, dissolve honey in warm water. Sprinkle yeast over the water and let it sit for about 5 minutes, until foamy.

2. In the bread machine pan, combine bread flour, chopped sage, salt, olive oil, and the yeast mixture.

3. Add mashed butternut squash on top of the flour mixture.

4. Place the bread machine pan into the machine. Select the "Whole Wheat" program and set crust shade and loaf size as desired. Press Start.

5. Once the bread is done, remove it from the bread machine and let it cool in the pan for 10 minutes. Then transfer it to a wire rack to cool completely before slicing.

Nutritional Value (Amount per Serving):

Calories: 266; Fat: 7.76; Carb: 42.19; Protein: 6.8

Bell Pepper and Onion Focaccia

Prep Time: 25 Minutes　　Cook Time: 3 Hours　　Serves: 8

Ingredients:

- 1 large bell pepper, thinly sliced
- 1 onion, thinly sliced
- 3 cups bread flour
- 2 teaspoons active dry yeast
- 1 teaspoon salt
- 1/4 cup olive oil, plus more for drizzling
- 1 1/4 cups warm water (110°F)

- Coarse sea salt, for sprinkling

Directions:

1. In a small bowl, dissolve salt in warm water. Sprinkle yeast over the water and let it sit for about 5 minutes, until foamy.
2. In the bread machine pan, combine bread flour, olive oil, and the yeast mixture.
3. Add thinly sliced bell pepper and onion on top of the flour mixture.
4. Place the bread machine pan into the machine. Select the "Artisan Dough" program and set crust shade and loaf size as desired. Press Start.
5. Once the dough is done, remove it from the bread machine and transfer it to a lightly oiled baking sheet.
6. Press the dough out into a rectangle or round shape, about 1/2 inch thick.
7. Cover the dough with a clean kitchen towel and let it rise in a warm place for about 30-45 minutes, until slightly puffed.
8. Preheat the oven to 400°F. Drizzle olive oil over the top of the focaccia and sprinkle with coarse sea salt.
9. Bake the focaccia for 20-25 minutes, until golden brown and crispy on the edges.
10. Remove the focaccia from the oven and let it cool on the baking sheet for 5 minutes. Then transfer it to a wire rack to cool completely before slicing.

Nutritional Value (Amount per Serving):

Calories: 282; Fat: 10.55; Carb: 37.78; Protein: 8.33

Beet and Goat Cheese Bread

Prep Time: 25 Minutes   Cook Time: 3 Hours   Serves: 8

Ingredients:

- 1 cup grated beets
- 1/2 cup crumbled goat cheese
- 3 cups bread flour
- 2 teaspoons active dry yeast
- 1 teaspoon salt
- 1 tablespoon honey
- 1/4 cup olive oil
- 1/4 cup warm water (110°F)

Directions:

1. In a small bowl, dissolve honey in warm water. Sprinkle yeast over the water and let it sit for about 5 minutes, until foamy.
2. In the bread machine pan, combine bread flour, salt, olive oil, and the yeast mixture.
3. Add grated beets and crumbled goat cheese on top of the flour mixture.
4. Place the bread machine pan into the machine. Select the "Artisan Dough" program and set crust shade and loaf size as desired. Press Start.
5. Once the dough is done, remove it from the bread machine and transfer it to a lightly floured surface.

6. Punch down the dough and shape it into a loaf. Place the loaf into a greased loaf pan.
7. Cover the loaf pan with a clean kitchen towel and let it rise in a warm place for about 30-45 minutes, until doubled in size.
8. Preheat the oven to 375°F. Bake the bread for 25-30 minutes, until golden brown and hollow-sounding when tapped on the bottom.
9. Remove the bread from the oven and let it cool in the pan for 10 minutes. Then transfer it to a wire rack to cool completely before slicing.

Nutritional Value (Amount per Serving):

Calories: 339; Fat: 12.75; Carb: 44.76; Protein: 11.12

Caramelized Onion and Gruyere Bread

Prep Time: 35 Minutes   Cook Time: 3 Hours   Serves: 8

Ingredients:

- 1 cup caramelized onions
- 1/2 cup grated Gruyere cheese
- 3 cups bread flour
- 2 teaspoons active dry yeast
- 1 teaspoon salt
- 1 tablespoon olive oil
- 1 cup warm water (110°F)

Directions:

1. In a small bowl, dissolve salt in warm water. Sprinkle yeast over the water and let it sit for about 5 minutes, until foamy.
2. In the bread machine pan, combine bread flour, olive oil, and the yeast mixture.
3. Add caramelized onions and grated Gruyere cheese on top of the flour mixture.
4. Place the bread machine pan into the machine. Select the "Artisan Dough" program and set crust shade and loaf size as desired. Press Start.
5. Once the dough is done, remove it from the bread machine and transfer it to a lightly floured surface.
6. Punch down the dough and shape it into a loaf. Place the loaf into a greased loaf pan.
7. Cover the loaf pan with a clean kitchen towel and let it rise in a warm place for about 30-45 minutes, until doubled in size.
8. Preheat the oven to 375°F. Bake the bread for 25-30 minutes, until golden brown and hollow-sounding when tapped on the bottom.
9. Remove the bread from the oven and let it cool in the pan for 10 minutes. Then transfer it to a wire rack to cool completely before slicing.

Nutritional Value (Amount per Serving):

Calories: 243; Fat: 5.3; Carb: 39.05; Protein: 9.18

Chapter 7: Rice Flour Gluten-free Breads

Sunflower Seed Rice Flour Bread

Prep Time: 15 Minutes   Cook Time: 3 Hours 30 Minutes   Serves: 8

Ingredients:

- 2 cups white rice flour
- 1/4 cup tapioca flour
- 1/4 cup potato starch
- 1 tablespoon active dry yeast
- 1 teaspoon xanthan gum
- 1 teaspoon salt
- 2 tablespoons honey
- 2 large eggs
- 1/4 cup olive oil
- 1 1/4 cups warm water
- 1/2 cup sunflower seeds

Directions:

1. In a large mixing bowl, combine white rice flour, tapioca flour, potato starch, yeast, xanthan gum, and salt.
2. In a separate bowl, whisk together honey, eggs, olive oil, and warm water until well combined.
3. Pour the wet ingredients into the dry ingredients and mix until a smooth batter forms.
4. Fold in sunflower seeds until evenly distributed.
5. Grease a loaf pan and pour the batter into it, smoothing the top with a spatula.
6. Place the loaf pan into the Cuisinart Bread Machine.
7. Select the Gluten-Free program, set the crust shade and loaf size as desired, then press Start.
8. Once the bread is done, remove it from the bread machine and let it cool in the pan for 10 minutes. Then transfer it to a wire rack to cool completely before slicing.

Nutritional Value (Amount per Serving):

Calories: 316; Fat: 13.07; Carb: 44.9; Protein: 5.65

Chia Seed Rice Flour Bread

Prep Time: 20 Minutes   Cook Time: 3 Hours 15 Minutes   Serves: 8

Ingredients:

- 2 cups white rice flour
- 1/4 cup tapioca flour
- 1/4 cup potato starch
- 1 tablespoon active dry yeast
- 1 teaspoon xanthan gum
- 1 teaspoon salt
- 2 tablespoons honey
- 2 large eggs
- 1/4 cup olive oil
- 1 1/4 cups warm water
- 1/4 cup chia seeds

Directions:

1. In a large mixing bowl, combine white rice flour, tapioca flour, potato starch, yeast, xanthan gum, and salt.
2. In a separate bowl, whisk together honey, eggs, olive oil, and warm water until well combined.
3. Pour the wet ingredients into the dry ingredients and mix until a smooth batter forms.
4. Fold in chia seeds until evenly distributed.
5. Grease a loaf pan and pour the batter into it, smoothing the top with a spatula.
6. Place the loaf pan into the Cuisinart Bread Machine.
7. Select the Gluten-Free program, set the crust shade and loaf size as desired, then press Start.
8. Once the bread is done, remove it from the bread machine and let it cool in the pan for 10 minutes. Then transfer it to a wire rack to cool completely before slicing.

Nutritional Value (Amount per Serving):

Calories: 300; Fat: 10.75; Carb: 46.14; Protein: 5

Pumpkin Seed Rice Flour Bread

Prep Time: 15 Minutes   Cook Time: 3 Hours 30 Minutes   Serves: 8

Ingredients:

- 2 cups white rice flour
- 1/4 cup tapioca flour
- 1/4 cup potato starch
- 1 tablespoon active dry yeast
- 1 teaspoon xanthan gum
- 1 teaspoon salt
- 2 tablespoons honey
- 2 large eggs
- 1/4 cup olive oil
- 1 1/4 cups warm water
- 1/2 cup pumpkin seeds

Directions:

1. In a large mixing bowl, combine white rice flour, tapioca flour, potato starch, yeast, xanthan gum, and salt.
2. In a separate bowl, whisk together honey, eggs, olive oil, and warm water until well combined.
3. Pour the wet ingredients into the dry ingredients and mix until a smooth batter forms.
4. Fold in pumpkin seeds until evenly distributed.
5. Grease a loaf pan and pour the batter into it, smoothing the top with a spatula.
6. Place the loaf pan into the Cuisinart Bread Machine.

7. Select the Gluten-Free program, set the crust shade and loaf size as desired, then press Start.
8. Once the bread is done, remove it from the bread machine and let it cool in the pan for 10 minutes. Then transfer it to a wire rack to cool completely before slicing.

Nutritional Value (Amount per Serving):

Calories: 308; Fat: 12.18; Carb: 44.24; Protein: 6.03

Cranberry Orange Rice Flour Bread

Prep Time: 20 Minutes   Cook Time: 3 Hours 15 Minutes   Serves: 8

Ingredients:

- 2 cups white rice flour
- 1/4 cup tapioca flour
- 1/4 cup potato starch
- 1 tablespoon active dry yeast
- 1 teaspoon xanthan gum
- 1 teaspoon salt
- Zest of 1 orange
- 1/2 cup dried cranberries
- 2 tablespoons honey
- 2 large eggs
- 1/4 cup olive oil
- 1 1/4 cups warm water

Directions:

1. In a large mixing bowl, combine white rice flour, tapioca flour, potato starch, yeast, xanthan gum, and salt.
2. In a separate bowl, whisk together honey, eggs, olive oil, and warm water until well combined.
3. Pour the wet ingredients into the dry ingredients and mix until a smooth batter forms.
4. Fold in orange zest and dried cranberries until evenly distributed.
5. Grease a loaf pan and pour the batter into it, smoothing the top with a spatula.
6. Place the loaf pan into the Cuisinart Bread Machine.
7. Select the Gluten-Free program, set the crust shade and loaf size as desired, then press Start.
8. Once the bread is done, remove it from the bread machine and let it cool in the pan for 10 minutes. Then transfer it to a wire rack to cool completely before slicing.

Nutritional Value (Amount per Serving):

Calories: 289; Fat: 8.62; Carb: 48.88; Protein: 4.04

Cranberry Walnut Rice Flour Bread

Prep Time: 20 Minutes   Cook Time: 3 Hours 15 Minutes   Serves: 8

Ingredients:

- 2 cups white rice flour
- 1/4 cup tapioca flour
- 1/4 cup potato starch
- 1 tablespoon active dry yeast
- 1 teaspoon xanthan gum
- 1 teaspoon salt
- 1/2 cup dried cranberries
- 1/2 cup chopped walnuts
- 2 tablespoons honey
- 2 large eggs
- 1/4 cup olive oil
- 1 1/4 cups warm water

Directions:

1. In a large mixing bowl, combine white rice flour, tapioca flour, potato starch, yeast, xanthan gum, and salt.
2. In a separate bowl, whisk together honey, eggs, olive oil, and warm water until well combined.
3. Pour the wet ingredients into the dry ingredients and mix until a smooth batter forms.
4. Fold in dried cranberries and chopped walnuts until evenly distributed.
5. Grease a loaf pan and pour the batter into it, smoothing the top with a spatula.
6. Place the loaf pan into the Cuisinart Bread Machine.
7. Select the Gluten-Free program, set the crust shade and loaf size as desired, then press Start.
8. Once the bread is done, remove it from the bread machine and let it cool in the pan for 10 minutes. Then transfer it to a wire rack to cool completely before slicing.

Nutritional Value (Amount per Serving):

Calories: 307; Fat: 11.84; Carb: 45.98; Protein: 4.59

Coconut Lime Rice Flour Bread

Prep Time: 15 Minutes   Cook Time: 3 Hours 30 Minutes   Serves: 8

Ingredients:

- 2 cups white rice flour
- 1/4 cup tapioca flour
- 1/4 cup potato starch
- 1 tablespoon active dry yeast
- 1 teaspoon xanthan gum
- 1 teaspoon salt
- Zest of 2 limes
- 1/2 cup shredded coconut
- 2 tablespoons honey
- 2 large eggs
- 1/4 cup olive oil
- 1 1/4 cups warm water

Directions:

1. In a large mixing bowl, combine white rice flour, tapioca flour, potato starch, yeast, xanthan gum, and salt.

2. In a separate bowl, whisk together honey, eggs, olive oil, and warm water until well combined.
3. Pour the wet ingredients into the dry ingredients and mix until a smooth batter forms.
4. Fold in lime zest and shredded coconut until evenly distributed.
5. Grease a loaf pan and pour the batter into it, smoothing the top with a spatula.
6. Place the loaf pan into the Cuisinart Bread Machine.
7. Select the Gluten-Free program, set the crust shade and loaf size as desired, then press Start.
8. Once the bread is done, remove it from the bread machine and let it cool in the pan for 10 minutes. Then transfer it to a wire rack to cool completely before slicing.

Nutritional Value (Amount per Serving):

Calories: 271; Fat: 8.6; Carb: 44.63; Protein: 3.99

Carrot Raisin Rice Flour Bread

Prep Time: 20 Minutes   Cook Time: 3 Hours 15 Minutes   Serves: 8

Ingredients:

- 2 cups white rice flour
- 1/4 cup tapioca flour
- 1/4 cup potato starch
- 1 tablespoon active dry yeast
- 1 teaspoon xanthan gum
- 1 teaspoon salt
- 1/2 cup grated carrots
- 1/2 cup raisins
- 2 tablespoons honey
- 2 large eggs
- 1/4 cup olive oil
- 1 1/4 cups warm water

Directions:

1. In a large mixing bowl, combine white rice flour, tapioca flour, potato starch, yeast, xanthan gum, and salt.
2. In a separate bowl, whisk together honey, eggs, olive oil, and warm water until well combined.
3. Pour the wet ingredients into the dry ingredients and mix until a smooth batter forms.
4. Fold in grated carrots and raisins until evenly distributed.
5. Grease a loaf pan and pour the batter into it, smoothing the top with a spatula.
6. Place the loaf pan into the Cuisinart Bread Machine.
7. Select the Gluten-Free program, set the crust shade and loaf size as desired, then press Start.
8. Once the bread is done, remove it from the bread machine and let it cool

in the pan for 10 minutes. Then transfer it to a wire rack to cool completely before slicing.

Nutritional Value (Amount per Serving):

Calories: 268; Fat: 8.58; Carb: 43.84; Protein: 3.9

Savory Herb Bread

Prep Time: 15 Minutes   Cook Time: 3 Hours   Serves: 8

Ingredients:

- 2 cups white rice flour
- 1/4 cup tapioca flour
- 1/4 cup potato starch
- 1 tablespoon active dry yeast
- 1 teaspoon xanthan gum
- 1 teaspoon salt
- 1 teaspoon dried basil
- 1 teaspoon dried oregano

- 1/2 teaspoon garlic powder
- 1/2 teaspoon onion powder
- 1/4 cup grated Parmesan cheese (optional)
- 2 tablespoons honey
- 2 large eggs
- 1/4 cup olive oil
- 1 1/4 cups warm water

Directions:

1. In a large mixing bowl, combine white rice flour, tapioca flour, potato starch, yeast, xanthan gum, salt, dried basil, dried oregano, garlic powder, onion powder, and grated Parmesan cheese.
2. In a separate bowl, whisk together honey, eggs, olive oil, and warm water until well combined.
3. Pour the wet ingredients into the dry ingredients and mix until smooth.
4. Grease a loaf pan and pour the batter into it, smoothing the top with a spatula.
5. Place the loaf pan into the Cuisinart Bread Machine.
6. Select the Gluten-Free program, set the crust shade and loaf size as desired, then press Start.
7. Once the bread is done, remove it from the bread machine and let it cool in the pan for 10 minutes. Then transfer it to a wire rack to cool completely before slicing.

Nutritional Value (Amount per Serving):

Calories: 280; Fat: 9.45; Carb: 43.98; Protein: 4.8

Herbed Garlic Bread

Prep Time: 15 Minutes   Cook Time: 3 Hours   Serves: 8

Ingredients:

- 2 cups white rice flour
- 1/4 cup tapioca flour
- 1/4 cup potato starch
- 1 tablespoon active dry yeast
- 1 teaspoon xanthan gum
- 1 teaspoon salt
- 1 teaspoon dried parsley
- 1 teaspoon dried thyme
- 1/2 teaspoon garlic powder
- 1/4 teaspoon onion powder
- 1/4 teaspoon dried rosemary
- 2 tablespoons honey
- 2 large eggs
- 1/4 cup olive oil
- 1 1/4 cups warm water

Directions:

1. In a large mixing bowl, combine white rice flour, tapioca flour, potato starch, yeast, xanthan gum, salt, dried parsley, dried thyme, garlic powder, onion powder, and dried rosemary.
2. In a separate bowl, whisk together honey, eggs, olive oil, and warm water until well combined.
3. Pour the wet ingredients into the dry ingredients and mix until smooth.
4. Grease a loaf pan and pour the batter into it, smoothing the top with a spatula.
5. Place the loaf pan into the Cuisinart Bread Machine.
6. Select the Gluten-Free program, set the crust shade and loaf size as desired, then press Start.
7. Once the bread is done, remove it from the bread machine and let it cool in the pan for 10 minutes. Then transfer it to a wire rack to cool completely before slicing.

Nutritional Value (Amount per Serving):

Calories: 266; Fat: 8.57; Carb: 43.4; Protein: 3.88

Seeded Rice Flour Bread

Prep Time: 15 Minutes   Cook Time: 3 Hours   Serves: 8

Ingredients:

- 1 1/2 cups white rice flour
- 1/2 cup tapioca flour
- 1/4 cup potato starch
- 1 tablespoon active dry yeast
- 1 teaspoon xanthan gum
- 1 teaspoon salt
- 1/4 cup sunflower seeds
- 1/4 cup pumpkin seeds
- 1/4 cup sesame seeds
- 2 tablespoons honey
- 2 large eggs
- 1/4 cup olive oil
- 1 1/4 cups warm water

Directions:

1. In a large mixing bowl, combine white rice flour, tapioca flour, potato starch, yeast, xanthan gum, salt, sunflower seeds, pumpkin seeds, and

sesame seeds.

2. In a separate bowl, whisk together honey, eggs, olive oil, and warm water until well combined.
3. Pour the wet ingredients into the dry ingredients and mix until smooth.
4. Grease a loaf pan and pour the batter into it, smoothing the top with a spatula.
5. Place the loaf pan into the Cuisinart Bread Machine.
6. Select the Gluten-Free program, set the crust shade and loaf size as desired, then press Start.
7. Once the bread is done, remove it from the bread machine and let it cool in the pan for 10 minutes. Then transfer it to a wire rack to cool completely before slicing.

Nutritional Value (Amount per Serving):

Calories: 322; Fat: 15.36; Carb: 41.42; Protein: 6.22

Herb and Cheese Rice Flour Bread

Prep Time: 20 Minutes   Cook Time: 3 Hours   Serves: 8

Ingredients:

- 2 cups white rice flour
- 1/4 cup tapioca flour
- 1/4 cup potato starch
- 1 tablespoon active dry yeast
- 1 teaspoon xanthan gum
- 1 teaspoon salt
- 1 teaspoon dried basil
- 1 teaspoon dried oregano
- 1/2 teaspoon garlic powder
- 1/4 cup grated Parmesan cheese
- 2 tablespoons honey
- 2 large eggs
- 1/4 cup olive oil
- 1 1/4 cups warm water

Directions:

1. In a large mixing bowl, combine white rice flour, tapioca flour, potato starch, yeast, xanthan gum, salt, dried basil, dried oregano, garlic powder, and grated Parmesan cheese.
2. In a separate bowl, whisk together honey, eggs, olive oil, and warm water until well combined.
3. Pour the wet ingredients into the dry ingredients and mix until smooth.
4. Grease a loaf pan and pour the batter into it, smoothing the top with a spatula.
5. Place the loaf pan into the Cuisinart Bread Machine.
6. Select the Gluten-Free program, set the crust shade and loaf size as desired, then press Start.
7. Once the bread is done, remove it from the bread machine and let it cool in the pan for 10 minutes. Then transfer it to a wire rack to cool completely before slicing.

Nutritional Value (Amount per Serving):

Calories: 280; Fat: 9.45; Carb: 43.86; Protein: 4.78

Chapter 8: Cheese Breads

Feta and Olive Bread

Prep Time: 20 Minutes   Cook Time: 3 Hours 30 Minutes   Serves: 8

Ingredients:

- 1 cup crumbled feta cheese
- 1/2 cup chopped Kalamata olives
- 3 cups bread flour
- 1 teaspoon salt
- 1 tablespoon sugar
- 1 packet (2 1/4 teaspoons) active dry yeast
- 1 cup warm water
- 2 tablespoons olive oil
- 1 large egg

Directions:

1. In a small bowl, mix together the crumbled feta cheese and chopped Kalamata olives. Set aside.
2. In the bread machine pan, add the bread flour, salt, sugar, and active dry yeast. Stir to combine.
3. Add the warm water and olive oil to the dry ingredients in the bread machine pan.
4. Select the "Artisan Dough" program on the Cuisinart Bread Machine and press Start.
5. Once the dough cycle is complete, remove the dough from the bread machine and place it on a lightly floured surface. Punch it down and knead it a few times.
6. Roll out the dough into a rectangle, about 1/2 inch thick. Sprinkle the feta cheese and olive mixture evenly over the dough.
7. Starting from one short end, roll the dough into a tight log. Pinch the seams to seal.
8. Place the dough seam side down in a greased loaf pan.
9. Cover the loaf pan with a clean kitchen towel and let the dough rise in a warm place for about 30 minutes, or until doubled in size.
10. Preheat the oven to 375°F. Beat the egg and brush it over the risen dough.
11. Bake the bread in the preheated oven for 30-35 minutes, or until golden brown and cooked through.
12. Remove the bread from the oven and let it cool in the pan for 10 minutes before transferring it to a wire rack to cool completely. Slice and serve.

Nutritional Value (Amount per Serving):

Calories: 288; Fat: 9.75; Carb: 40; Protein: 9.59

Parmesan and Garlic Bread

Prep Time: 15 Minutes   Cook Time: 3 Hours 30 Minutes   Serves: 8

Ingredients:

- 1 cup grated Parmesan cheese
- 3 cloves garlic, minced
- 3 cups bread flour
- 1 teaspoon salt
- 1 tablespoon sugar
- 1 packet (2 1/4 teaspoons) active dry yeast
- 1 cup warm water
- 2 tablespoons olive oil
- 1 large egg

Directions:

1. In a small bowl, mix together the grated Parmesan cheese and minced garlic. Set aside.
2. In the bread machine pan, add the bread flour, salt, sugar, and active dry yeast. Stir to combine.
3. Add the warm water and olive oil to the dry ingredients in the bread machine pan.
4. Select the "Artisan Dough" program on the Cuisinart Bread Machine and press Start.
5. Once the dough cycle is complete, remove the dough from the bread machine and place it on a lightly floured surface. Punch it down and knead it a few times.
6. Roll out the dough into a rectangle, about 1/2 inch thick. Sprinkle the Parmesan cheese and garlic mixture evenly over the dough.
7. Starting from one short end, roll the dough into a tight log. Pinch the seams to seal.
8. Place the dough seam side down in a greased loaf pan.
9. Cover the loaf pan with a clean kitchen towel and let the dough rise in a warm place for about 30 minutes, or until doubled in size.
10. Preheat the oven to 375°F. Beat the egg and brush it over the risen dough.
11. Bake the bread in the preheated oven for 30-35 minutes, or until golden brown and cooked through.
12. Remove the bread from the oven and let it cool in the pan for 10 minutes before transferring it to a wire rack to cool completely. Slice and serve.

Nutritional Value (Amount per Serving):

Calories: 283; Fat: 8.35; Carb: 40.82; Protein: 10.48

Swiss and Ham Bread

Prep Time: 20 Minutes   Cook Time: 3 Hours 30 Minutes   Serves: 8

Ingredients:

- 1 cup shredded Swiss cheese
- 1/2 cup diced ham
- 3 cups bread flour
- 1 teaspoon salt
- 1 tablespoon sugar
- 1 packet (2 1/4 teaspoons) active dry yeast
- 1 cup warm water
- 2 tablespoons olive oil
- 1 large egg

Directions:

1. In a small bowl, mix together the shredded Swiss cheese and diced ham. Set aside.
2. In the bread machine pan, add the bread flour, salt, sugar, and active dry yeast. Stir to combine.
3. Add the warm water and olive oil to the dry ingredients in the bread machine pan.
4. Select the "Artisan Dough" program on the Cuisinart Bread Machine and press Start.
5. Once the dough cycle is complete, remove the dough from the bread machine and place it on a lightly floured surface. Punch it down and knead it a few times.
6. Roll out the dough into a rectangle, about 1/2 inch thick. Sprinkle the Swiss cheese and ham mixture evenly over the dough.
7. Starting from one short end, roll the dough into a tight log. Pinch the seams to seal.
8. Place the dough seam side down in a greased loaf pan.
9. Cover the loaf pan with a clean kitchen towel and let the dough rise in a warm place for about 30 minutes, or until doubled in size.
10. Preheat the oven to 375°F. Beat the egg and brush it over the risen dough.
11. Bake the bread in the preheated oven for 30-35 minutes, or until golden brown and cooked through.
12. Remove the bread from the oven and let it cool in the pan for 10 minutes before transferring it to a wire rack to cool completely. Slice and serve.

Nutritional Value (Amount per Serving):

Calories: 306; Fat: 9.93; Carb: 39.73; Protein: 13.69

Mozzarella and Sun-Dried Tomato Bread

Prep Time: 20 Minutes   Cook Time: 3 Hours 30 Minutes   Serves: 8

Ingredients:

- 1 cup shredded mozzarella cheese
- 1/2 cup chopped sun-dried tomatoes (drained if packed in oil)
- 3 cups bread flour
- 1 teaspoon salt
- 1 tablespoon sugar
- 1 packet (2 1/4 teaspoons) active dry yeast
- 1 cup warm water
- 2 tablespoons olive oil
- 1 large egg

Directions:

1. In a small bowl, mix together the shredded mozzarella cheese and chopped sun-dried tomatoes. Set aside.
2. In the bread machine pan, add the bread flour, salt, sugar, and active dry yeast. Stir to combine.
3. Add the warm water and olive oil to the dry ingredients in the bread machine pan.
4. Select the "Artisan Dough" program on the Cuisinart Bread Machine and press Start.
5. Once the dough cycle is complete, remove the dough from the bread machine and place it on a lightly floured surface. Punch it down and knead it a few times.
6. Roll out the dough into a rectangle, about 1/2 inch thick. Sprinkle the mozzarella cheese and sun-dried tomato mixture evenly over the dough.
7. Starting from one short end, roll the dough into a tight log. Pinch the seams to seal.
8. Place the dough seam side down in a greased loaf pan.
9. Cover the loaf pan with a clean kitchen towel and let the dough rise in a warm place for about 30 minutes, or until doubled in size.
10. Preheat the oven to 375°F. Beat the egg and brush it over the risen dough.
11. Bake the bread in the preheated oven for 30-35 minutes, or until golden brown and cooked through.
12. Remove the bread from the oven and let it cool in the pan for 10 minutes before transferring it to a wire rack to cool completely. Slice and serve.

Nutritional Value (Amount per Serving):

Calories: 258; Fat: 4.96; Carb: 41.08; Protein: 11.81

Gruyère and Caramelized Onion Bread

Prep Time: 25 Minutes   Cook Time: 3 Hours 30 Minutes   Serves: 8

Ingredients:

- 1 cup shredded Gruyère cheese
- 1 large onion, thinly sliced
- 2 tablespoons butter
- 3 cups bread flour
- 1 teaspoon salt
- 1 tablespoon sugar
- 1 packet (2 1/4 teaspoons) active dry yeast
- 1 cup warm water
- 2 tablespoons olive oil
- 1 large egg

Directions:

1. In a skillet, melt the butter over medium heat. Add the thinly sliced onion and cook, stirring occasionally, until caramelized, about 15-20 minutes. Set aside to cool.
2. In the bread machine pan, add the bread flour, salt, sugar, and active dry yeast. Stir to combine.
3. Add the warm water and olive oil to the dry ingredients in the bread machine pan.
4. Select the "Artisan Dough" program on the Cuisinart Bread Machine and press Start.
5. Once the dough cycle is complete, remove the dough from the bread machine and place it on a lightly floured surface. Punch it down and knead it a few times.
6. Roll out the dough into a rectangle, about 1/2 inch thick. Spread the caramelized onions evenly over the dough, then sprinkle the shredded Gruyère cheese on top.
7. Starting from one short end, roll the dough into a tight log. Pinch the seams to seal.
8. Place the dough seam side down in a greased loaf pan.
9. Cover the loaf pan with a clean kitchen towel and let the dough rise in a warm place for about 30 minutes, or until doubled in size.
10. Preheat the oven to 375°F. Beat the egg and brush it over the risen dough.
11. Bake the bread in the preheated oven for 30-35 minutes, or until golden brown and cooked through.
12. Remove the bread from the oven and let it cool in the pan for 10 minutes before transferring it to a wire rack to cool completely. Slice and serve.

Nutritional Value (Amount per Serving):

Calories: 366; Fat: 17.11; Carb: 39.16; Protein: 13.15

Provolone and Basil Bread

Prep Time: 20 Minutes   Cook Time: 3 Hours 30 Minutes   Serves: 8

Ingredients:

- 1 cup shredded provolone cheese
- 1/4 cup chopped fresh basil
- 3 cups bread flour
- 1 teaspoon salt
- 1 tablespoon sugar
- 1 packet (2 1/4 teaspoons) active dry yeast
- 1 cup warm water
- 2 tablespoons olive oil
- 1 large egg

Directions:

1. In a small bowl, mix together the shredded provolone cheese and chopped fresh basil. Set aside.
2. In the bread machine pan, add the bread flour, salt, sugar, and active dry yeast. Stir to combine.
3. Add the warm water and olive oil to the dry ingredients in the bread machine pan.
4. Select the "Artisan Dough" program on the Cuisinart Bread Machine and press Start.
5. Once the dough cycle is complete, remove the dough from the bread machine and place it on a lightly floured surface. Punch it down and knead it a few times.
6. Roll out the dough into a rectangle, about 1/2 inch thick. Sprinkle the provolone cheese and basil mixture evenly over the dough.
7. Starting from one short end, roll the dough into a tight log. Pinch the seams to seal.
8. Place the dough seam side down in a greased loaf pan.
9. Cover the loaf pan with a clean kitchen towel and let the dough rise in a warm place for about 30 minutes, or until doubled in size.
10. Preheat the oven to 375°F. Beat the egg and brush it over the risen dough.
11. Bake the bread in the preheated oven for 30-35 minutes, or until golden brown and cooked through.
12. Remove the bread from the oven and let it cool in the pan for 10 minutes before transferring it to a wire rack to cool completely. Slice and serve.

Nutritional Value (Amount per Serving):

Calories: 287; Fat: 9.26; Carb: 39.08; Protein: 11.1

Havarti and Dill Bread

Prep Time: 20 Minutes   Cook Time: 3 Hours 30 Minutes   Serves: 8

Ingredients:

- 1 cup shredded Havarti cheese
- 2 tablespoons chopped fresh dill
- 3 cups bread flour
- 1 teaspoon salt
- 1 tablespoon sugar
- 1 packet (2 1/4 teaspoons) active dry yeast
- 1 cup warm water
- 2 tablespoons olive oil
- 1 large egg

Directions:

1. In a small bowl, mix together the shredded Havarti cheese and chopped fresh dill. Set aside.
2. In the bread machine pan, add the bread flour, salt, sugar, and active dry yeast. Stir to combine.
3. Add the warm water and olive oil to the dry ingredients in the bread machine pan.
4. Select the "Artisan Dough" program on the Cuisinart Bread Machine and press Start.
5. Once the dough cycle is complete, remove the dough from the bread machine and place it on a lightly floured surface. Punch it down and knead it a few times.
6. Roll out the dough into a rectangle, about 1/2 inch thick. Sprinkle the Havarti cheese and dill mixture evenly over the dough.
7. Starting from one short end, roll the dough into a tight log. Pinch the seams to seal.
8. Place the dough seam side down in a greased loaf pan.
9. Cover the loaf pan with a clean kitchen towel and let the dough rise in a warm place for about 30 minutes, or until doubled in size.
10. Preheat the oven to 375°F. Beat the egg and brush it over the risen dough.
11. Bake the bread in the preheated oven for 30-35 minutes, or until golden brown and cooked through.
12. Remove the bread from the oven and let it cool in the pan for 10 minutes before transferring it to a wire rack to cool completely. Slice and serve.

Nutritional Value (Amount per Serving):

Calories: 295; Fat: 10; Carb: 40.08; Protein: 10.95

Fontina and Pesto Bread

Prep Time: 20 Minutes   Cook Time: 3 Hours 30 Minutes   Serves: 8

Ingredients:

- 1 cup shredded Fontina cheese
- 1/4 cup prepared pesto sauce
- 3 cups bread flour
- 1 teaspoon salt
- 1 tablespoon sugar
- 1 packet (2 1/4 teaspoons) active dry yeast
- 1 cup warm water
- 2 tablespoons olive oil
- 1 large egg

Directions:

1. In a small bowl, mix together the shredded Fontina cheese and prepared pesto sauce. Set aside.
2. In the bread machine pan, add the bread flour, salt, sugar, and active dry yeast. Stir to combine.
3. Add the warm water and olive oil to the dry ingredients in the bread machine pan.
4. Select the "Artisan Dough" program on the Cuisinart Bread Machine and press Start.
5. Once the dough cycle is complete, remove the dough from the bread machine and place it on a lightly floured surface. Punch it down and knead it a few times.
6. Roll out the dough into a rectangle, about 1/2 inch thick. Sprinkle the Fontina cheese and pesto mixture evenly over the dough.
7. Starting from one short end, roll the dough into a tight log. Pinch the seams to seal.
8. Place the dough seam side down in a greased loaf pan.
9. Cover the loaf pan with a clean kitchen towel and let the dough rise in a warm place for about 30 minutes, or until doubled in size.
10. Preheat the oven to 375°F. Beat the egg and brush it over the risen dough.
11. Bake the bread in the preheated oven for 30-35 minutes, or until golden brown and cooked through.
12. Remove the bread from the oven and let it cool in the pan for 10 minutes before transferring it to a wire rack to cool completely. Slice and serve.

Nutritional Value (Amount per Serving):

Calories: 335; Fat: 14.25; Carb: 39.27; Protein: 11.84

Ricotta and Spinach Bread

Prep Time: 25 Minutes   Cook Time: 3 Hours 30 Minutes   Serves: 8

Ingredients:

- 1 cup ricotta cheese
- 1/2 cup chopped cooked spinach (squeeze out excess moisture)
- 3 cups bread flour
- 1 teaspoon salt
- 1 tablespoon sugar
- 1 packet (2 1/4 teaspoons) active dry yeast
- 1 cup warm water
- 2 tablespoons olive oil
- 1 large egg

Directions:

1. In a small bowl, mix together the ricotta cheese and chopped cooked spinach. Set aside.
2. In the bread machine pan, add the bread flour, salt, sugar, and active dry yeast. Stir to combine.
3. Add the warm water and olive oil to the dry ingredients in the bread machine pan.
4. Select the "Artisan Dough" program on the Cuisinart Bread Machine and press Start.
5. Once the dough cycle is complete, remove the dough from the bread machine and place it on a lightly floured surface. Punch it down and knead it a few times.
6. Roll out the dough into a rectangle, about 1/2 inch thick. Spread the ricotta and spinach mixture evenly over the dough.
7. Starting from one short end, roll the dough into a tight log. Pinch the seams to seal.
8. Place the dough seam side down in a greased loaf pan.
9. Cover the loaf pan with a clean kitchen towel and let the dough rise in a warm place for about 30 minutes, or until doubled in size.
10. Preheat the oven to 375°F. Beat the egg and brush it over the risen dough.
11. Bake the bread in the preheated oven for 30-35 minutes, or until golden brown and cooked through.
12. Remove the bread from the oven and let it cool in the pan for 10 minutes before transferring it to a wire rack to cool completely. Slice and serve.

Nutritional Value (Amount per Serving):

Calories: 285; Fat: 8.91; Carb: 40.07; Protein: 10.68

Chapter 9: Sweet Breads

Maple Pecan Bread

Prep Time: 20 Minutes   Cook Time: 3 Hours   Serves: 8

Ingredients:

- 1 1/2 cups all-purpose flour
- 1 teaspoon baking powder
- 1/2 teaspoon baking soda
- 1/4 teaspoon salt
- 1/2 cup unsalted butter, softened
- 3/4 cup pure maple syrup
- 2 large eggs
- 1 teaspoon vanilla extract
- 1/2 cup chopped pecans

Directions:

1. In a bowl, whisk together flour, baking powder, baking soda, and salt.
2. In another bowl, cream together softened butter and maple syrup until light and fluffy.
3. Beat in eggs, one at a time, then stir in vanilla extract.
4. Gradually add the dry ingredients to the wet ingredients, mixing until just combined.
5. Fold in chopped pecans.
6. Grease a loaf pan and pour the batter into it, smoothing the top with a spatula.
7. Place the loaf pan into the Cuisinart Bread Machine.
8. Select the Cake program and set crust shade and loaf size as desired. Press Start.
9. Once the bread is done, remove it from the bread machine and let it cool in the pan for 10 minutes. Then transfer it to a wire rack to cool completely before slicing.

Nutritional Value (Amount per Serving):

Calories: 291; Fat: 13.55; Carb: 39.06; Protein: 4.14

Marbled Chocolate Banana Bread

Prep Time: 20 Minutes   Cook Time: 3 Hours   Serves: 8

Ingredients:

- 1 1/2 cups all-purpose flour
- 1 teaspoon baking powder
- 1/2 teaspoon baking soda
- 1/4 teaspoon salt
- 1/2 cup unsalted butter, softened
- 3/4 cup granulated sugar
- 2 large eggs
- 1 teaspoon vanilla extract
- 3 ripe bananas, mashed
- 1/4 cup unsweetened cocoa powder
- 1/4 cup hot water

Directions:

1. In a bowl, whisk together flour, baking powder, baking soda, and salt.

2. In another bowl, cream together softened butter and sugar until light and fluffy.
3. Beat in eggs, one at a time, then stir in vanilla extract and mashed bananas.
4. Gradually add the dry ingredients to the wet ingredients, mixing until just combined.
5. In a small bowl, mix cocoa powder with hot water until smooth.
6. Pour half of the banana batter into a separate bowl and mix in the cocoa mixture.
7. Alternate spoonfuls of the plain and chocolate batters into a greased loaf pan.
8. Use a knife to gently swirl the batters together to create a marbled effect.
9. Place the loaf pan into the Cuisinart Bread Machine.
10. Select the Cake program and set crust shade and loaf size as desired. Press Start.
11. Once the bread is done, remove it from the bread machine and let it cool in the pan for 10 minutes. Then transfer it to a wire rack to cool completely before slicing.

Nutritional Value (Amount per Serving):

Calories: 264; Fat: 11.61; Carb: 37.5; Protein: 4.43

Raspberry Lemon Bread

Prep Time: 20 Minutes   Cook Time: 3 Hours   Serves: 8

Ingredients:

- 1 1/2 cups all-purpose flour
- 1 teaspoon baking powder
- 1/2 teaspoon baking soda
- 1/4 teaspoon salt
- 1/2 cup unsalted butter, softened
- 3/4 cup granulated sugar
- 2 large eggs
- Zest of 1 lemon
- 1/4 cup fresh lemon juice
- 1/2 cup plain yogurt
- 1 cup fresh raspberries

Directions:

1. In a bowl, whisk together flour, baking powder, baking soda, and salt.
2. In another bowl, cream together softened butter and sugar until light and fluffy.
3. Beat in eggs, one at a time, then stir in lemon zest, lemon juice, and yogurt.
4. Gradually add the dry ingredients to the wet ingredients, mixing until just combined.
5. Gently fold in fresh raspberries.
6. Grease a loaf pan and pour the batter into it, smoothing the top with a spatula.

7. Place the loaf pan into the Cuisinart Bread Machine.
8. Select the Cake program and set crust shade and loaf size as desired. Press Start.
9. Once the bread is done, remove it from the bread machine and let it cool in the pan for 10 minutes. Then transfer it to a wire rack to cool completely before slicing.

Nutritional Value (Amount per Serving):

Calories: 247; Fat: 9.64; Carb: 36.81; Protein: 4.4

Chocolate Cherry Bread

Prep Time: 20 Minutes   Cook Time: 3 Hours   Serves: 8

Ingredients:

- 1 1/2 cups all-purpose flour
- 1 teaspoon baking powder
- 1/2 teaspoon baking soda
- 1/4 teaspoon salt
- 1/2 cup unsalted butter, softened
- 3/4 cup granulated sugar
- 2 large eggs
- 1 teaspoon vanilla extract
- 1/2 cup unsweetened cocoa powder
- 1/4 cup hot water
- 1 cup cherries, pitted and chopped

Directions:

1. In a bowl, whisk together flour, baking powder, baking soda, and salt.
2. In another bowl, cream together softened butter and sugar until light and fluffy.
3. Beat in eggs, one at a time, then stir in vanilla extract.
4. Gradually add the dry ingredients to the wet ingredients, mixing until just combined.
5. In a small bowl, mix cocoa powder with hot water until smooth.
6. Add the cocoa mixture to the batter and mix until well combined.
7. Fold in chopped cherries.
8. Grease a loaf pan and pour the batter into it, smoothing the top with a spatula.
9. Place the loaf pan into the Cuisinart Bread Machine.
10. Select the Cake program and set crust shade and loaf size as desired. Press Start.
11. Once the bread is done, remove it from the bread machine and let it cool in the pan for 10 minutes. Then transfer it to a wire rack to cool completely before slicing.

Nutritional Value (Amount per Serving):

Calories: 230; Fat: 9.81; Carb: 33.61; Protein: 4.77

Coconut Pineapple Bread

Prep Time: 20 Minutes   Cook Time: 3 Hours   Serves: 8

Ingredients:

- 1 1/2 cups all-purpose flour
- 1 teaspoon baking powder
- 1/2 teaspoon baking soda
- 1/4 teaspoon salt
- 1/2 cup unsalted butter, softened
- 3/4 cup granulated sugar
- 2 large eggs
- 1 teaspoon vanilla extract
- 1/2 cup canned crushed pineapple, drained
- 1/2 cup shredded coconut

Directions:

1. In a bowl, whisk together flour, baking powder, baking soda, and salt.
2. In another bowl, cream together softened butter and sugar until light and fluffy.
3. Beat in eggs, one at a time, then stir in vanilla extract.
4. Gradually add the dry ingredients to the wet ingredients, mixing until just combined.
5. Fold in crushed pineapple and shredded coconut.
6. Grease a loaf pan and pour the batter into it, smoothing the top with a spatula.
7. Place the loaf pan into the Cuisinart Bread Machine.
8. Select the Cake program and set crust shade and loaf size as desired. Press Start.
9. Once the bread is done, remove it from the bread machine and let it cool in the pan for 10 minutes. Then transfer it to a wire rack to cool completely before slicing.

Nutritional Value (Amount per Serving):

Calories: 220; Fat: 9.12; Carb: 30.75; Protein: 3.73

Chocolate Chip Zucchini Bread

Prep Time: 20 Minutes   Cook Time: 3 Hours   Serves: 8

Ingredients:

- 1 1/2 cups all-purpose flour
- 1 teaspoon baking powder
- 1/2 teaspoon baking soda
- 1/2 teaspoon salt
- 1 teaspoon ground cinnamon
- 2 large eggs

- 1/2 cup vegetable oil
- 3/4 cup granulated sugar
- 1 teaspoon vanilla extract
- 1 cup shredded zucchini, squeezed dry
- 1/2 cup semi-sweet chocolate chips

Directions:

1. In a bowl, whisk together flour, baking powder, baking soda, salt, and cinnamon.
2. In another bowl, beat eggs, then stir in vegetable oil, sugar, and vanilla extract.
3. Gradually add the dry ingredients to the wet ingredients, mixing until just combined.
4. Fold in shredded zucchini and chocolate chips.
5. Grease a loaf pan and pour the batter into it, smoothing the top with a spatula.
6. Place the loaf pan into the Cuisinart Bread Machine.
7. Select the Cake program and set crust shade and loaf size as desired. Press Start.
8. Once the bread is done, remove it from the bread machine and let it cool in the pan for 10 minutes. Then transfer it to a wire rack to cool completely before slicing.

Nutritional Value (Amount per Serving):

Calories: 328; Fat: 19.84; Carb: 36.62; Protein: 3.7

Chocolate Marble Bread

Prep Time: 20 Minutes   Cook Time: 3 Hours   Serves: 8

Ingredients:

- 1 1/2 cups all-purpose flour
- 1 teaspoon baking powder
- 1/2 teaspoon baking soda
- 1/4 teaspoon salt
- 1/4 cup unsweetened cocoa powder
- 1/4 cup hot water
- 1/2 cup unsalted butter, softened
- 3/4 cup granulated sugar
- 2 large eggs
- 1 teaspoon vanilla extract
- 1/2 cup milk

Directions:

1. In a small bowl, mix cocoa powder with hot water until smooth. Let it cool.
2. In another bowl, whisk together flour, baking powder, baking soda, and salt.
3. In a separate large bowl, cream together softened butter and sugar until light and fluffy.

4. Beat in eggs, one at a time, then stir in vanilla extract.
5. Gradually add the dry ingredients to the wet ingredients, alternating with milk, mixing until just combined.
6. Divide the batter in half. Mix the cocoa mixture into one half.
7. Grease a loaf pan and pour alternate spoonfuls of vanilla and chocolate batter into it.
8. Use a knife to gently swirl the batters together to create a marble effect.
9. Place the loaf pan into the Cuisinart Bread Machine.
10. Select the Cake program and set crust shade and loaf size as desired. Press Start.
11. Once the bread is done, remove it from the bread machine and let it cool in the pan for 10 minutes. Then transfer it to a wire rack to cool completely before slicing.

Nutritional Value (Amount per Serving):

Calories: 223; Fat: 9.93; Carb: 30.05; Protein: 4.52

Lemon Poppy Seed Bread

Prep Time: 20 Minutes   Cook Time: 3 Hours   Serves: 8

Ingredients:

- 1 1/2 cups all-purpose flour
- 1 teaspoon baking powder
- 1/2 teaspoon baking soda
- 1/4 teaspoon salt
- Zest of 2 lemons
- 2 tablespoons poppy seeds
- 1/2 cup unsalted butter, softened
- 3/4 cup granulated sugar
- 2 large eggs
- 1/2 cup plain yogurt
- 1/4 cup fresh lemon juice
- 1 teaspoon vanilla extract

Directions:

1. In a bowl, whisk together flour, baking powder, baking soda, salt, lemon zest, and poppy seeds.
2. In another bowl, cream together softened butter and sugar until light and fluffy.
3. Beat in eggs, one at a time, then stir in yogurt, lemon juice, and vanilla extract.
4. Gradually add the dry ingredients to the wet ingredients, mixing until just combined.
5. Grease a loaf pan and pour the batter into it, smoothing the top with a spatula.
6. Place the loaf pan into the Cuisinart Bread Machine.
7. Select the Cake program and set crust shade and loaf size as desired. Press Start.

8. Once the bread is done, remove it from the bread machine and let it cool in the pan for 10 minutes. Then transfer it to a wire rack to cool completely before slicing.

Nutritional Value (Amount per Serving):

Calories: 233; Fat: 10.53; Carb: 30.44; Protein: 4.55

Chocolate Swirl Bread

Prep Time: 20 Minutes   Cook Time: 3 Hours   Serves: 8

Ingredients:

- 2 cups all-purpose flour
- 1/4 cup unsweetened cocoa powder
- 1 teaspoon baking powder
- 1/2 teaspoon baking soda
- 1/2 teaspoon salt
- 1/2 cup unsalted butter, softened
- 1 cup granulated sugar
- 2 large eggs
- 1 teaspoon vanilla extract
- 1 cup buttermilk
- 1/2 cup semi-sweet chocolate chips, melted

Directions:

1. In a bowl, whisk together flour, cocoa powder, baking powder, baking soda, and salt.
2. In another bowl, cream together softened butter and sugar until light and fluffy.
3. Beat in eggs, one at a time, then stir in vanilla extract.
4. Gradually add the dry ingredients to the wet ingredients, alternating with buttermilk, mixing until just combined.
5. Grease a loaf pan and pour half of the batter into it, smoothing the top with a spatula.
6. Drizzle melted chocolate over the batter in the pan, then pour the remaining batter on top.
7. Use a knife to swirl the chocolate into the batter.
8. Place the loaf pan into the Cuisinart Bread Machine.
9. Select the Cake program and set crust shade and loaf size as desired. Press Start.
10. Once the bread is done, remove it from the bread machine and let it cool in the pan for 10 minutes. Then transfer it to a wire rack to cool completely before slicing.

Nutritional Value (Amount per Serving):

Calories: 338; Fat: 14.62; Carb: 48.43; Protein: 6.42

Blueberry Lemon Bread

Prep Time: 20 Minutes   Cook Time: 3 Hours   Serves: 8

Ingredients:

- 1 1/2 cups all-purpose flour
- 1 teaspoon baking powder
- 1/2 teaspoon baking soda
- 1/4 teaspoon salt
- 1/2 cup unsalted butter, softened
- 1 cup granulated sugar
- 2 large eggs
- 1 teaspoon vanilla extract
- 1/2 cup plain yogurt
- Zest of 1 lemon
- 1 cup fresh blueberries

Directions:

1. In a bowl, whisk together flour, baking powder, baking soda, and salt.
2. In another bowl, cream together softened butter and sugar until light and fluffy.
3. Beat in eggs, one at a time, then stir in vanilla extract.
4. Gradually add the dry ingredients to the wet ingredients, alternating with yogurt, mixing until just combined.
5. Fold in lemon zest and fresh blueberries.
6. Grease a loaf pan and pour the batter into it, smoothing the top with a spatula.
7. Place the loaf pan into the Cuisinart Bread Machine.
8. Select the Cake program and set crust shade and loaf size as desired. Press Start.
9. Once the bread is done, remove it from the bread machine and let it cool in the pan for 10 minutes. Then transfer it to a wire rack to cool completely before slicing.

Nutritional Value (Amount per Serving):

Calories: 258; Fat: 9.69; Carb: 39.06; Protein: 4.32

Chapter 10: Grain-free Gluten-free Breads

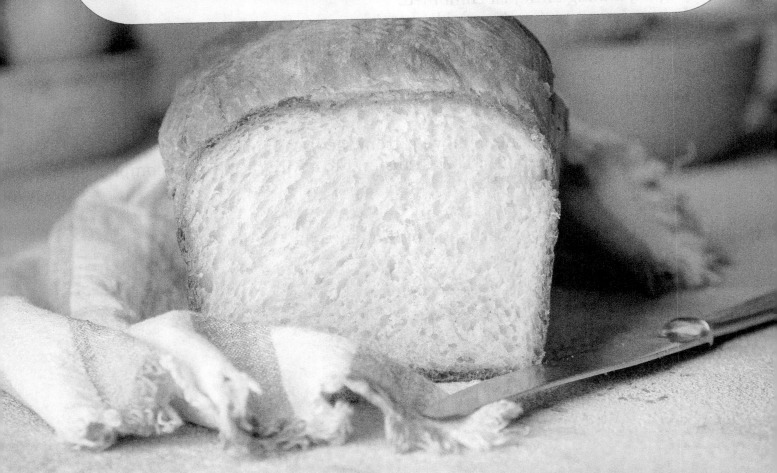

Flaxseed Coconut Bread

Prep Time: 20 Minutes   Cook Time: 3 Hours   Serves: 8

Ingredients:

- 1 1/2 cups ground flaxseed
- 1/2 cup coconut flour
- 1/4 cup almond flour
- 1 tsp baking powder
- 1/2 tsp baking soda
- 1/2 tsp salt
- 4 large eggs
- 1/4 cup coconut oil, melted
- 1/4 cup unsweetened almond milk
- 2 tbsp apple cider vinegar

Directions:

1. In a large mixing bowl, combine ground flaxseed, coconut flour, almond flour, baking powder, baking soda, and salt.
2. In another bowl, whisk together eggs, melted coconut oil, almond milk, and apple cider vinegar until well combined.
3. Pour the wet ingredients into the dry ingredients and mix until smooth.
4. Grease a loaf pan and pour the batter into it, spreading evenly.
5. Place the loaf pan into the Cuisinart Bread Machine.
6. Select the Gluten-Free program and set the crust shade and loaf size according to your preference. Press Start.
7. Once the bread is done baking, carefully remove the loaf pan from the machine and allow it to cool for 10 minutes before transferring the bread to a wire rack to cool completely. Slice and serve.

Nutritional Value (Amount per Serving):

Calories: 263; Fat: 22.49; Carb: 11; Protein: 7.27

Hazelnut Meal Bread

Prep Time: 20 Minutes   Cook Time: 3 Hours   Serves: 8

Ingredients:

- 1 1/2 cups hazelnut meal
- 1/2 cup almond flour
- 1/4 cup coconut flour
- 1 tsp baking soda
- 1/2 tsp salt
- 4 large eggs
- 1/4 cup coconut oil, melted
- 1/4 cup unsweetened almond milk
- 2 tbsp apple cider vinegar

Directions:

1. In a large mixing bowl, combine hazelnut meal, almond flour, coconut flour, baking soda, and salt.
2. In another bowl, whisk together eggs, melted coconut oil, almond milk, and apple cider vinegar until well combined.

3. Pour the wet ingredients into the dry ingredients and mix until smooth.
4. Grease a loaf pan and pour the batter into it, spreading evenly.
5. Place the loaf pan into the Cuisinart Bread Machine.
6. Select the Gluten-Free program and set the crust shade and loaf size according to your preference. Press Start.
7. Once the bread is done baking, carefully remove the loaf pan from the machine and allow it to cool for 10 minutes before transferring the bread to a wire rack to cool completely. Slice and serve.

Nutritional Value (Amount per Serving):

Calories: 251; Fat: 24.59; Carb: 5.56; Protein: 5.25

Chia Seed Bread

Prep Time: 20 Minutes   Cook Time: 3 Hours   Serves: 8

Ingredients:

- 1 1/2 cups almond flour
- 1/2 cup coconut flour
- 1/4 cup chia seeds
- 1 tsp baking powder
- 1/2 tsp baking soda

- 1/2 tsp salt
- 4 large eggs
- 1/4 cup coconut oil, melted
- 1/4 cup unsweetened almond milk
- 2 tbsp apple cider vinegar

Directions:

1. In a large mixing bowl, combine almond flour, coconut flour, chia seeds, baking powder, baking soda, and salt.
2. In another bowl, whisk together eggs, melted coconut oil, almond milk, and apple cider vinegar until well combined.
3. Pour the wet ingredients into the dry ingredients and mix until smooth.
4. Grease a loaf pan and pour the batter into it, spreading evenly.
5. Place the loaf pan into the Cuisinart Bread Machine.
6. Select the Gluten-Free program and set the crust shade and loaf size according to your preference. Press Start.
7. Once the bread is done baking, carefully remove the loaf pan from the machine and allow it to cool for 10 minutes before transferring the bread to a wire rack to cool completely. Slice and serve.

Nutritional Value (Amount per Serving):

Calories: 130; Fat: 11.49; Carb: 4.93; Protein: 2.72

Walnut Flour Bread

Prep Time: 20 Minutes   Cook Time: 3 Hours   Serves: 8

Ingredients:

- 1 1/2 cups walnut flour
- 1/2 cup almond flour
- 1/4 cup coconut flour
- 1 tsp baking soda
- 1/2 tsp salt
- 4 large eggs
- 1/4 cup coconut oil, melted
- 1/4 cup unsweetened almond milk
- 2 tbsp apple cider vinegar

Directions:

1. In a large mixing bowl, combine walnut flour, almond flour, coconut flour, baking soda, and salt.
2. In another bowl, whisk together eggs, melted coconut oil, almond milk, and apple cider vinegar until well combined.
3. Pour the wet ingredients into the dry ingredients and mix until smooth.
4. Grease a loaf pan and pour the batter into it, spreading evenly.
5. Place the loaf pan into the Cuisinart Bread Machine.
6. Select the Gluten-Free program and set the crust shade and loaf size according to your preference. Press Start.
7. Once the bread is done baking, carefully remove the loaf pan from the machine and allow it to cool for 10 minutes before transferring the bread to a wire rack to cool completely. Slice and serve.

Nutritional Value (Amount per Serving):

Calories: 191; Fat: 19; Carb: 3.39; Protein: 3.75

Chestnut Flour Bread

Prep Time: 20 Minutes   Cook Time: 3 Hours   Serves: 8

Ingredients:

- 1 1/2 cups chestnut flour
- 1/2 cup almond flour
- 1/4 cup coconut flour
- 1 tsp baking powder
- 1/2 tsp baking soda
- 1/2 tsp salt
- 4 large eggs
- 1/4 cup coconut oil, melted
- 1/4 cup unsweetened almond milk
- 2 tbsp apple cider vinegar

Directions:

1. In a large mixing bowl, combine chestnut flour, almond flour, coconut flour, baking powder, baking soda, and salt.
2. In another bowl, whisk together eggs, melted coconut oil, almond milk, and apple cider vinegar until well combined.
3. Pour the wet ingredients into the dry ingredients and mix until smooth.
4. Grease a loaf pan and pour the batter into it, spreading evenly.
5. Place the loaf pan into the Cuisinart Bread Machine.

6. Select the Gluten-Free program and set the crust shade and loaf size according to your preference. Press Start.
7. Once the bread is done baking, carefully remove the loaf pan from the machine and allow it to cool for 10 minutes before transferring the bread to a wire rack to cool completely. Slice and serve.

Nutritional Value (Amount per Serving):

Calories: 151; Fat: 9.83; Carb: 14.03; Protein: 2.12

Pecan Meal Bread

Prep Time: 20 Minutes   Cook Time: 3 Hours   Serves: 8

Ingredients:

- 1 1/2 cups pecan meal
- 1/2 cup almond flour
- 1/4 cup coconut flour
- 1 tsp baking soda
- 1/2 tsp salt
- 4 large eggs
- 1/4 cup coconut oil, melted
- 1/4 cup unsweetened almond milk
- 2 tbsp apple cider vinegar

Directions:

1. In a large mixing bowl, combine pecan meal, almond flour, coconut flour, baking soda, and salt.
2. In another bowl, whisk together eggs, melted coconut oil, almond milk, and apple cider vinegar until well combined.
3. Pour the wet ingredients into the dry ingredients and mix until smooth.
4. Grease a loaf pan and pour the batter into it, spreading evenly.
5. Place the loaf pan into the Cuisinart Bread Machine.
6. Select the Gluten-Free program and set the crust shade and loaf size according to your preference. Press Start.
7. Once the bread is done baking, carefully remove the loaf pan from the machine and allow it to cool for 10 minutes before transferring the bread to a wire rack to cool completely. Slice and serve.

Nutritional Value (Amount per Serving):

Calories: 221; Fat: 22.57; Carb: 3.91; Protein: 3.17

Hemp Seed Bread

Prep Time: 20 Minutes   Cook Time: 3 Hours   Serves: 8

Ingredients:

- 1 1/2 cups almond flour
- 1/2 cup coconut flour

- 1/4 cup hemp seeds
- 1 tsp baking powder
- 1/2 tsp baking soda
- 1/2 tsp salt

- 4 large eggs
- 1/4 cup coconut oil, melted
- 1/4 cup unsweetened almond milk
- 2 tbsp apple cider vinegar

Directions:

1. In a large mixing bowl, combine almond flour, coconut flour, hemp seeds, baking powder, baking soda, and salt.
2. In another bowl, whisk together eggs, melted coconut oil, almond milk, and apple cider vinegar until well combined.
3. Pour the wet ingredients into the dry ingredients and mix until smooth.
4. Grease a loaf pan and pour the batter into it, spreading evenly.
5. Place the loaf pan into the preheated Cuisinart Bread Machine.
6. Select the Gluten-Free program and set the crust shade and loaf size according to your preference. Press Start.
7. Once the bread is done baking, carefully remove the loaf pan from the machine and allow it to cool for 10 minutes before transferring the bread to a wire rack to cool completely. Slice and serve.

Nutritional Value (Amount per Serving):

Calories: 121; Fat: 11.56; Carb: 2.82; Protein: 2.46

Tigernut Flour Bread

Prep Time: 20 Minutes   Cook Time: 3 Hours   Serves: 8

Ingredients:

- 1 1/2 cups tigernut flour
- 1/2 cup almond flour
- 1/4 cup coconut flour
- 1 tsp baking soda
- 1/2 tsp salt

- 4 large eggs
- 1/4 cup coconut oil, melted
- 1/4 cup unsweetened almond milk
- 2 tbsp apple cider vinegar

Directions:

1. In a large mixing bowl, combine tigernut flour, almond flour, coconut flour, baking soda, and salt.
2. In another bowl, whisk together eggs, melted coconut oil, almond milk, and apple cider vinegar until well combined.
3. Pour the wet ingredients into the dry ingredients and mix until smooth.
4. Grease a loaf pan and pour the batter into it, spreading evenly.
5. Place the loaf pan into the Cuisinart Bread Machine.
6. Select the Gluten-Free program and set the crust shade and loaf size according to your preference. Press Start.
7. Once the bread is done baking, carefully remove the loaf pan from the

machine and allow it to cool for 10 minutes before transferring the bread to a wire rack to cool completely. Slice and serve.

Nutritional Value (Amount per Serving):

Calories: 178; Fat: 9.44; Carb: 19.22; Protein: 3.89

Brazil Nut Flour Bread

Prep Time: 20 Minutes   Cook Time: 3 Hours   Serves: 8

Ingredients:

- 1 1/2 cups Brazil nut flour
- 1/2 cup almond flour
- 1/4 cup coconut flour
- 1 tsp baking powder
- 1/2 tsp baking soda

- 1/2 tsp salt
- 4 large eggs
- 1/4 cup coconut oil, melted
- 1/4 cup unsweetened almond milk
- 2 tbsp apple cider vinegar

Directions:

1. In a large mixing bowl, combine Brazil nut flour, almond flour, coconut flour, baking powder, baking soda, and salt.
2. In another bowl, whisk together eggs, melted coconut oil, almond milk, and apple cider vinegar until well combined.
3. Pour the wet ingredients into the dry ingredients and mix until smooth.
4. Grease a loaf pan and pour the batter into it, spreading evenly.
5. Place the loaf pan into the Cuisinart Bread Machine.
6. Select the Gluten-Free program and set the crust shade and loaf size according to your preference. Press Start.
7. Once the bread is done baking, carefully remove the loaf pan from the machine and allow it to cool for 10 minutes before transferring the bread to a wire rack to cool completely. Slice and serve.

Nutritional Value (Amount per Serving):

Calories: 257; Fat: 25.95; Carb: 4.56; Protein: 5.04

Cassava Flour Bread

Prep Time: 20 Minutes   Cook Time: 3 Hours   Serves: 8

Ingredients:

- 1 1/2 cups cassava flour
- 1/2 cup almond flour
- 1/4 cup coconut flour
- 1 tsp baking powder

- 1/2 tsp baking soda
- 1/2 tsp salt
- 4 large eggs
- 1/4 cup coconut oil, melted

- 1/4 cup unsweetened almond milk
- 2 tbsp apple cider vinegar

Directions:

1. In a large mixing bowl, combine cassava flour, almond flour, coconut flour, baking powder, baking soda, and salt.
2. In another bowl, whisk together eggs, melted coconut oil, almond milk, and apple cider vinegar until well combined.
3. Pour the wet ingredients into the dry ingredients and mix until smooth.
4. Grease a loaf pan and pour the batter into it, spreading evenly.
5. Place the loaf pan into the Cuisinart Bread Machine.
6. Select the Gluten-Free program and set the crust shade and loaf size according to your preference. Press Start.
7. Once the bread is done baking, carefully remove the loaf pan from the machine and allow it to cool for 10 minutes before transferring the bread to a wire rack to cool completely. Slice and serve.

Nutritional Value (Amount per Serving):

Calories: 155; Fat: 9.33; Carb: 16.33; Protein: 1.99

Chickpea Flour Bread

Prep Time: 20 Minutes   Cook Time: 3 Hours   Serves: 8

Ingredients:

- 1 1/2 cups chickpea flour
- 1/2 cup almond flour
- 1/4 cup coconut flour
- 1 tsp baking powder
- 1/2 tsp baking soda
- 1/2 tsp salt
- 4 large eggs
- 1/4 cup coconut oil, melted
- 1/4 cup unsweetened almond milk
- 2 tbsp apple cider vinegar

Directions:

1. In a large mixing bowl, combine chickpea flour, almond flour, coconut flour, baking powder, baking soda, and salt.
2. In another bowl, whisk together eggs, melted coconut oil, almond milk, and apple cider vinegar until well combined.
3. Pour the wet ingredients into the dry ingredients and mix until smooth.
4. Grease a loaf pan and pour the batter into it, spreading evenly.
5. Place the loaf pan into the Cuisinart Bread Machine.
6. Select the Gluten-Free program and set the crust shade and loaf size according to your preference. Press Start.
7. Once the bread is done baking, carefully remove the loaf pan from the machine and allow it to cool for 10 minutes before transferring the bread to a wire rack to cool completely. Slice and serve.

Nutritional Value (Amount per Serving):

Calories: 160; Fat: 10.37; Carb: 11.6; Protein: 5.33

Coconut Flour Banana Bread

Prep Time: 15 Minutes   Cook Time: 3 Hours   Serves: 8

Ingredients:

- 1 cup coconut flour
- 1 tsp baking soda
- 1/2 tsp salt
- 4 ripe bananas, mashed
- 6 large eggs
- 1/4 cup honey or maple syrup
- 1/4 cup coconut oil, melted
- 1 tsp vanilla extract
- Optional: 1/2 cup chopped nuts or chocolate chips

Directions:

1. In a large mixing bowl, combine coconut flour, baking soda, and salt.
2. In another bowl, mash the bananas thoroughly.
3. Add eggs, honey or maple syrup, melted coconut oil, and vanilla extract to the mashed bananas. Mix until well combined.
4. Pour the wet ingredients into the dry ingredients and mix until a smooth batter forms. If desired, fold in chopped nuts or chocolate chips.
5. Grease a loaf pan and pour the batter into it, spreading evenly.
6. Place the loaf pan into the Cuisinart Bread Machine.
7. Select the Gluten-Free program and set the crust shade and loaf size according to your preference. Press Start.
8. Once the bread is finished baking, carefully remove the loaf pan from the machine and allow it to cool for 10 minutes before transferring the bread to a wire rack to cool completely. Slice and serve.

Nutritional Value (Amount per Serving):

Calories: 270; Fat: 16.45; Carb: 28.8; Protein: 3.5

APPENDIX RECIPE INDEX

Made in the USA
Middletown, DE
02 September 2024

60292661R00064